How much do you know about outer space? What about sport, art, history, music, the world of film and television, books and nature? These are just *some* of the fascinating facts you'll have at your fingertips once you've delved into this book. And you'll find a few jokes too – so hurry up and get twentying!

Barbara Gilgallon and Sue Samuels are both experienced teachers, who have compiled a number of popular quiz books, including *The Calendar Quiz Book*, published in Puffin.

*Another book by the same authors*
**The Calendar Quiz Book**

BARBARA GILGALLON
*and* SUE SAMUELS

# The Twenty/Twenty Quiz Book

*illustrated by* JON MILLER

PUFFIN BOOKS

*For Chloe, Joel and Alex*

PUFFIN BOOKS

Published by the Penguin Group
27 Wrights Lane, London w8 5TZ, England
Viking Penguin Inc., 40 West 23rd Street, New York, New York 10010, USA
Penguin Books Australia Ltd, Ringwood, Victoria, Australia
Penguin Books Canada Ltd, 2801 John Street, Markham, Ontario, Canada L3R 1B4
Penguin Books (NZ) Ltd, 182–190 Wairau Road, Auckland 10, New Zealand

Penguin Books Ltd, Registered Offices: Harmondsworth, Middlesex, England

First published 1988

Text copyright © Barbara Gilgallon and Sue Samuels, 1988
Illustrations copyright © Jon Miller, 1988
All rights reserved

Typeset in 9/11pt Linotron 202 Palatino by
Rowland Phototypesetting Ltd, Bury St Edmunds, Suffolk
Made and printed in Great Britain by
Cox & Wyman Ltd, Reading

Except in the United States of America, this book is sold subject
to the condition that it shall not, by way of trade or otherwise, be lent,
re-sold, hired out, or otherwise circulated without the publisher's
prior consent in any form of binding or cover other than that in which
it is published and without a similar condition including this condition
being imposed on the subsequent purchaser

# Contents

1 Twenty Facts about Twenty
3 Hidden Treasure
6 Busman's Holiday?
7 Women of the World
8 Some 'Fantastic' Books
10 Feathered Friends
12 Piggy Bank Posers
14 The Wild West
16 Twenty Mixed-up Jokes
18 Driving Range
19 The Best of Enemies
20 Ready for Take-off
21 Men of the World
22 Twenty Questions for High Fliers
25 Royal Progress
27 Match the Music
28 Tree Word-search
30 Back to the Nursery
32 As Seen on TV
33 Criss-cross Words
34 Crack the Word

- 36 Arty-crafty
- 38 Twenty Running Questions
- 40 Twenty Jumping Questions
- 42 Twenty Standing Still Questions
- 44 My Word!
- 47 Heroes and Heroines
- 49 Twenty Fruit Facts
- 51 Characters in Search of a Bargain
- 52 Celebrations!
- 54 Beastly Books
- 56 Quick Change
- 57 Happy Families
- 58 For Your Bookshelf
- 60 Think Small
- 61 Larger than Life
- 63 Criss-cross Words
- 64 Pet Shop Posers
- 66 The Show Must Go On!
- 68 All Dressed Up
- 70 Come to the Concert
- 72 Twenty Superlative Questions
- 73 Through the Centuries
- 76 Tourist Attractions
- 78 Twenty 'Waiter, waiter' Jokes
- 80 Something Fishy
- 82 Oddities
- 83 Musical Beasts
- 84 Search Party

- 85 Don't Vegetate!
- 86 Dining Out
- 88 All in the Game
- 90 Togetherness
- 91 Find the Number
- 93 Get the Point?
- 94 Twenty Questions from Outer Space
- 96 Twenty 'Doctor, doctor' Jokes
- 99 Headline News
- 100 Up Front
- 101 A Quiz to Make You Tremble
- 106 For Wild Things
- 107 Mixed Doubles
- 108 Signs of the Times
- 110 A Winner Every Time
- 112 Let's Get Physical
- 114 Score Bored?
- 116 Twenty Bright Ideas
- 119 On Safari
- 121 Round the World
- 123 In Their Own Words

- 127 Answers

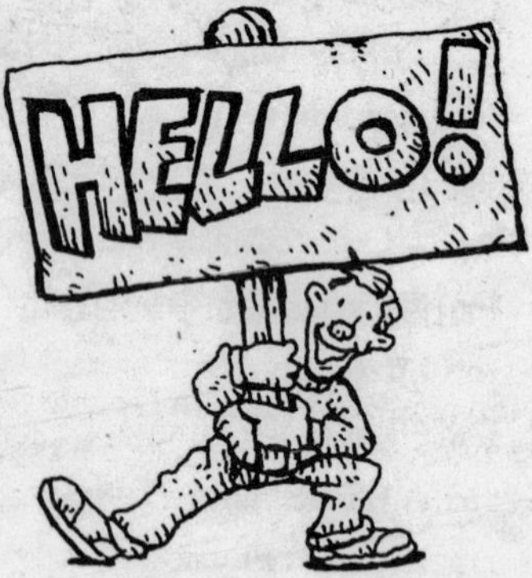
HELLO!

# 1 Twenty Facts about Twenty

1. Twenty is the name of a place in Lincolnshire.
2. The human brain is said to be at its best at twenty years.
3. Samuel Colt patented his famous revolver at the age of twenty . . .
4. . . . and Mary Shelley was also twenty when her book *Frankenstein* was published.
5. The body of the stegosaurus was about twenty times the size of his brain.
6. The average human male body is covered by about twenty square feet of skin.
7. The Maya tribe used a base of twenty for counting. This was because they used their toes as well as their fingers.
8. A twentieth wedding anniversary is celebrated with china – so everybody can have a smashing time!
9. Four weeks after her twentieth birthday, Lady Diana Spencer married Prince Charles.
10. On the other hand, Catherine Howard, the fifth wife of Henry VIII, was beheaded when she was twenty.
11. Adolf Hitler was born on 20 April 1889.
12. At the age of twenty males can expect to live for another fifty-one years and females for another fifty-three years.

13 · No such luck for the wild pig. His life expectancy is twenty years.
14 · Captain Scott was only twenty kilometres from safety when he died, returning from the South Pole.
15 · Twenty per cent of the earth's atmosphere is made up of oxygen.
16 · In 1904 nobody was allowed to drive at more than twenty m.p.h.
17 · The first charity walk took place on Boxing Day in 1959 and raised £20.
18 · Billie Jean King has won twenty Wimbledon titles: six singles, ten women's doubles and four mixed doubles.
19 · The longest serving British prime minister was Sir Robert Walpole, who served for 20 years and 326 days.
20 · The average iceberg weighs twenty tons.

## 2 Hidden Treasure

*Shiver me timbers! Avast there me hearties!*
*My treasure's safely buried, away from prying eyes,*
*And Iguana Island is where the booty lies.*
*But if you want to find it, each question is a clue,*
*The first letter of each answer will tell you what to do.*
            Signed: Cap'n Jollybeard

1. Everything King Midas touched turned to this.
2. The password Ali Baba used.
3. Long John Silver is in this book.
4. The shimmering colour of these stones is called opalescence.
5. A red jewel and a girl's name.
6. Translucent yellow 'stone' from fossilized pine tree resin.
7. The tomb of this Eygptian king was full of gold and treasure.
8. The Crown Jewels are kept here.
9. Dip into this tub of bran for a surprise gift.
10. Ireland is nicknamed after this green jewel.
11. The bells in Contrary Mary's garden.
12. Pendants, chains and chokers are types of this.

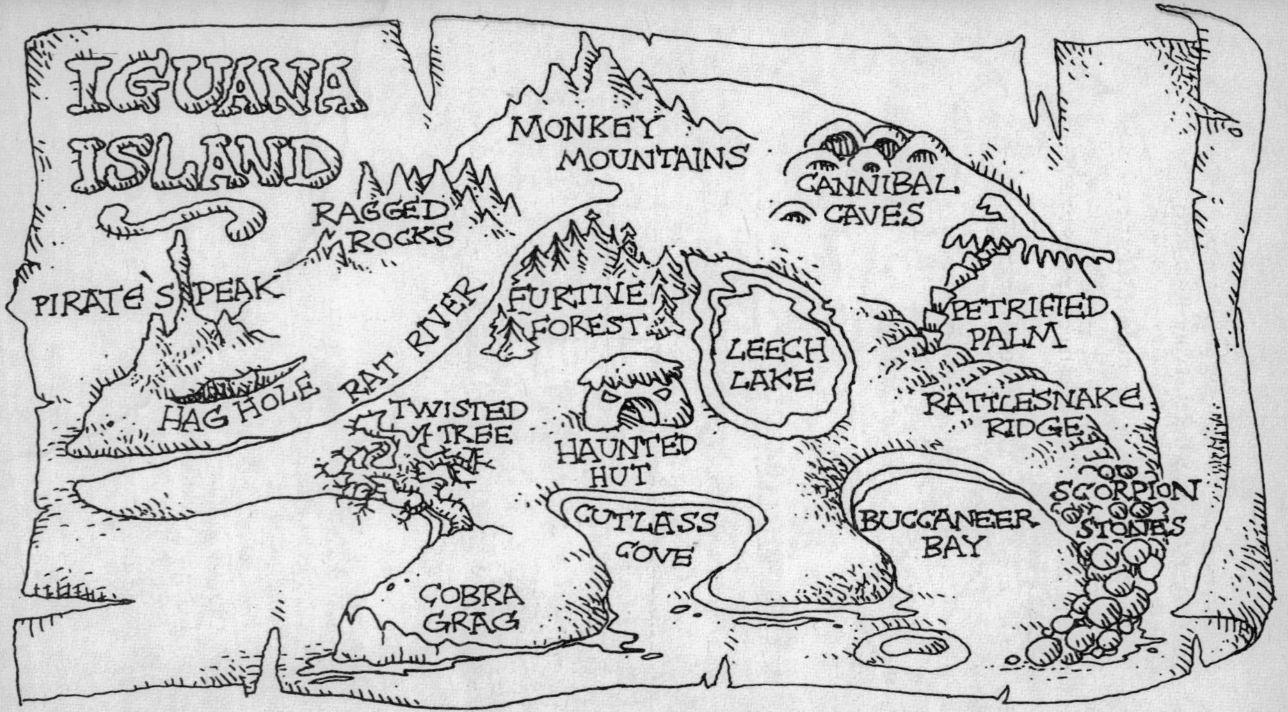
IGUANA ISLAND
MONKEY MOUNTAINS
CANNIBAL CAVES
RAGGED ROCKS
PIRATE'S PEAK
RAT RIVER
FURTIVE FOREST
LEECH LAKE
PETRIFIED PALM
HAG HOLE
TWISTED TREE
HAUNTED HUT
RATTLESNAKE RIDGE
CUTLASS COVE
BUCCANEER BAY
SCORPION STONES
COBRA CRAG

13 · He obtained riches by rubbing an old lamp.
14 · The strong American fort that contains much of the world's gold.
15 · In a Greek legend a goose produced these in pure gold.
16 · Finger jewellery.
17 · A precious creamy-white substance usually obtained from elephant tusks.
18 · These are for ever in a James Bond film.
19 · Precious stones of all sorts.
20 · The golden city of South American legend.

Put the first letters into this grid and the instructions will be revealed!

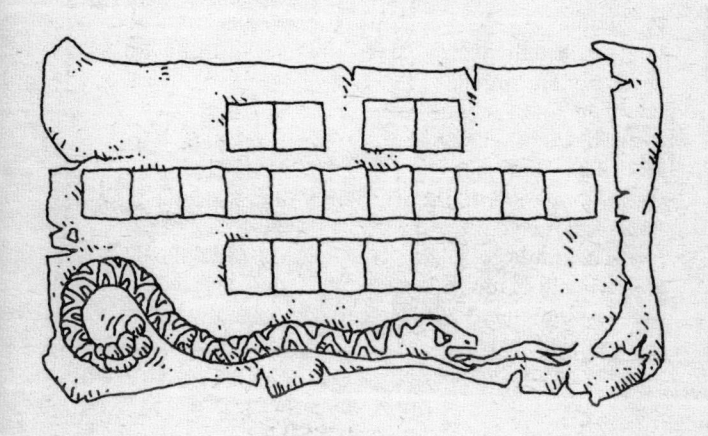

# 3 Busman's Holiday?

Nobody here queues at the bus-stop – they all ride in style.
Can you match the traveller to the transport?

1 · Dr Who
2 · Jonah
3 · Cinderella
4 · Dick Turpin
5 · The Owl and the Pussycat
6 · Han Solo
7 · Neil Armstrong
8 · Daisy
9 · James
10 · Richard Branson
11 · Thor Heyerdahl
12 · The Walker children
13 · The Pilgrim Fathers
14 · Susan and Lucy
15 · Commander Caractacus Potts
16 · Captain Nemo
17 · The Jumblies
18 · Donald Campbell
19 · Captain Bligh
20 · Butcher, baker, candlestickmaker

a sieve
*Virgin Atlantic*
the *Tardis*
a giant peach
a bicycle made for two
*Chitty-Chitty-Bang-Bang*
a whale
*Swallow*
*Nautilus*
a transformed pumpkin
*Apollo 11*
*Bluebird*
Black Bess
HMS *Bounty*
a pea-green boat
the *Millennium Falcon*
the *Mayflower*
Aslan the lion
*Kon-Tiki*
a tub

# 4 Women of the World

Each of these groups of women has one thing in common. Do you know what it is?

1. Tatum O'Neal, Shirley Temple, Judy Garland.
2. Mary Quant, Coco Chanel, Zandra Rhodes.
3. Maria Callas, Joan Sutherland, Kiri Te Kanawa.
4. Indira Gandhi, Golda Meir, Margaret Thatcher.
5. Mrs Beeton, Delia Smith, Sarah Brown.
6. Kate Greenaway, Nicola Bayley, Janet Ahlberg.
7. Cleopatra, Marie Antoinette, Elizabeth I.
8. Amelia Earhart, Amy Johnson, Sheila Scott.
9. Judy Blume, Joan Eadington, Enid Blyton.
10. Coppélia, Ragdolly Anna, Barbie.
11. Bangles, Amazulu, Bananarama.
12. Pat Smythe, Princess Anne, Lucinda Green.
13. Tessa Sanderson, Zola Budd, Rosie Ackermann.
14. Mary Pickford, Greta Garbo, Katharine Hepburn.
15. Janet Ellis, Caron Keating, Sarah Greene.
16. Cleo Laine, Billie Holiday, Marian Montgomery.
17. Pamela Stephenson, Tracey Ullman, Janet Brown.
18. Maggie Smith, Prunella Scales, Meryl Streep.
19. Anna Pavlova, Ginger Rogers, Isadora Duncan.
20. Kate Adie, Julia Somerville, Sue Lawley.

## 5 Some 'Fantastic' Books

These books are all linked by fantasy and imagination. Fill in the missing words in their titles and put them on the grid. When it is complete it will reveal the name of a fantastic form of transport.

1. \_ \_ \_ \_ \_ \_ \_ \_ \_ \_'\_ Web by E. B. White.
2. James and the Giant \_ \_ \_ \_ \_ by Roald Dahl.
3. The \_ \_ \_ \_ \_ \_ \_ of Earthsea by Ursula Le Guin.
4. \_ \_ \_ \_ Pan by J. M. Barrie.
5. Finn Family \_ \_ \_ \_ \_ \_ \_ \_ \_ \_ \_ \_ by Tove Jansson.
6. \_ \_ \_ \_ Poppins by Mary Travers.
7. \_ \_ \_ \_ \_ \_ \_ \_ \_ \_ \_ by Carlo Collodi.
8. The \_ \_ \_ \_ \_ \_ Prince by Oscar Wilde.
9. Dr \_ \_ \_ \_ \_ \_ \_ \_ \_ by Hugh Lofting.
10. Pippi \_ \_ \_ \_ \_ \_ \_ \_ \_ \_ \_ \_ \_ \_ by Astrid Lindgren.
11. Mrs \_ \_ \_ \_ \_ \_ \_ \_ \_ by Alf Prøysen.
12. The \_ \_ \_ \_ \_ \_ of the Dawn Treader by C. S. Lewis.
13. The Water \_ \_ \_ \_ \_ \_ by Charles Kingsley.

14. _ _ _ _ _ _ _ _ _ by Richard Carpenter.
15. Dot and the _ _ _ _ _ _ _ _ by Ethel C. Pedley.
16. The Box of _ _ _ _ _ _ _ _ by John Masefield.
17. The _ _ _ _ _ _ by J. R. Tolkien.
18. _ _ _ _ _'s Adventures in Wonderland by Lewis Carroll.
19. The Sword in the _ _ _ _ _ by T. H. White.
20. Tom's Midnight _ _ _ _ _ _ by Philippa Pearce.

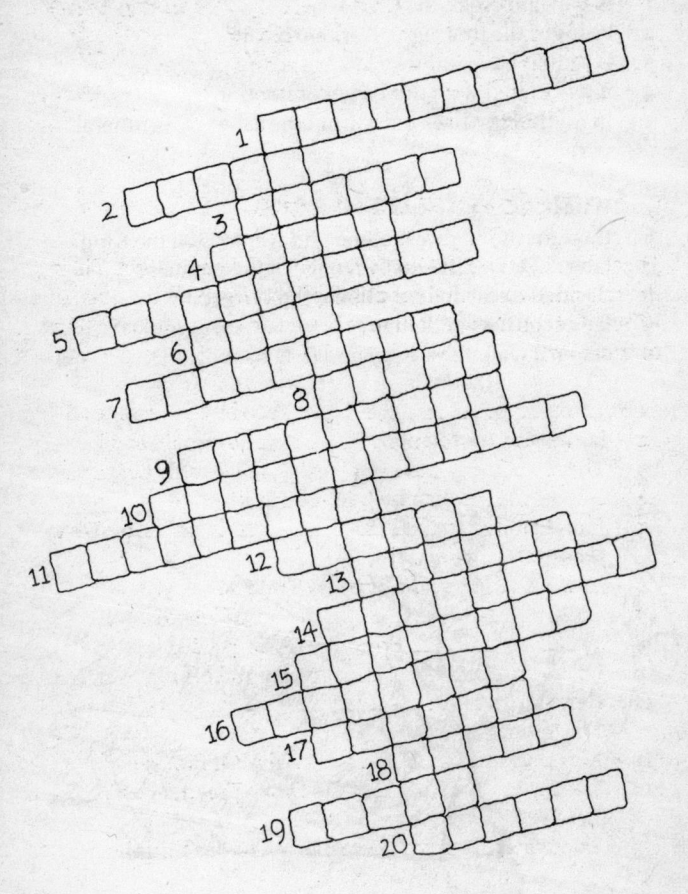

# 6 Feathered Friends

Feeling chirpy? All birdbrains should be able to whistle through these questions.

**Which bird . . .**
1 · is the emblem of the USA?
2 · brought the first sign of land to Noah?
3 · is said to have unlucky tail feathers?
4 · is associated with the Tower of London?
5 · in mythology rises anew from the ashes of its funeral pyre?

**Who . . .**
6 · thought the sky was falling and went to tell the King?
7 · taught Dr Dolittle the language of the animals?
8 · decided to call his new home the Wolery?
9 · lays eggs for gentlemen?
10 · sat on a wall, flew away and flew back again?

**Which or what . . .**
11 · is the largest living bird?
12 · birds lay eggs in other birds' nests?
13 · birds can fly forwards and backwards and hover?
14 · does a pelican use its pouch for?
15 · bird is the fastest creature on earth?

**True or False?**
16 · Birds don't have teeth.
17 · Birds moult.
18 · Feathers are warmer than fur.
19 · A bird's first breath of air is taken inside the egg.
20 · All birds can fly.

# 7 Piggy Bank Posers

How good are you with money? Do you hoard your pocket money or race to the nearest shop? These statements are all to do with money matters. Some are true and some are false. Can you sort them out?

1 · Florence Nightingale appears on the back of a £10 note.
2 · The first credit card was Diners Club.
3 · A 50p coin has eight edges.
4 · The word bank comes from the Italian for bench.
5 · The first banknote appeared in 1661.
6 · Everything that King Midas touched turned to silver.
7 · In nineteenth-century China bamboo was used for money.
8 · 2,000 years ago the Romans collected Greek coins.
9 · Dolphins' teeth are used for currency in the Solomon Islands.
10 · Income tax was introduced to pay for the war against Napoleon.
11 · The US treasury produces 80,000,000 coins per year.
12 · British money became decimalized in 1971.

13 · Piggy banks were based on pig farms.
14 · The word billionaire was first used in 1861.
15 · Banknotes in Britain are signed by the prime minister.
16 · Britannia first appeared on a Roman coin in the time of the Emperor Hadrian.
17 · Paper money was invented by the Chinese.
18 · The currency of Portugal is the peseta.
19 · In America there are more than 1,000,000 millionaires.
20 · The American millionairess Hetty Howland Green ate cold porridge because it would cost more to heat it!

## 8 The Wild West

Are you wild about the West? Here are some rootin' tootin' questions for all you sons of a gun!

1. Calamity Jane was christened
   a) Martha Jane Canary
   b) Sarah Jane Cuckoo
   c) Emily Jane Swift.
2. John 'Doc' Holliday was a
   a) gunfighting doctor
   b) gunfighting vet
   c) gunfighting dentist.
3. Judge Roy Bean dispensed justice from
   a) a saloon bar called the 'Jersey Lily'
   b) a paddle-steamer called the 'Water Lily'
   c) a park called the 'Lily of the Valley'.
4. Tom Smith, marshal of Abilene, kept order with
   a) his karate kicks
   b) his six-gun
   c) his sledgehammer fists.

5. The Iron Horse was
   a) Sitting Bull's famous steed
   b) the Indians' name for the locomotive
   c) an electric bucking bronco.
6. Pay dirt was
   a) earth that contained gold
   b) money won at cards
   c) money stolen by outlaws.

**Which of these Western facts are true and which are false?**

7. A chuck wagon contained all the rubbish of the wagon train.
8. Branding irons were used for shaping cowboy hats.
9. Billy the Kid escaped from prison with a gun hidden for him in the toilet.
10. An Indian reservation is a group booking for the wagon train.
11. The outlaw Butch Cassidy was once a butcher.
12. Henry Wells and William Fargo built up a great network of paddle-steamers.
13. Louisiana Territory was purchased from France for about $15,000,000.
14. Custer's last stand was the Battle of Little Big Horn.
15. The population of Guthrie, Oklahoma, grew from nought to 10,000 in a month.
16. Pony Express riders had to be under eighteen.
17. The Forty-niners were a band of forty-nine-year-old outlaws.
18. Wyatt Earp took part in the gunfight at the OK Corral.
19. Indians used totem poles for building their tepees.
20. Annie Oakley could shoot out the pips on a playing card at thirty paces.

# 9 Twenty Mixed-up Jokes

What do you get if you cross . . .

1 · a giraffe with a hedgehog?
   *A tall toothbrush.*

2 · an elephant with a computer?
   *A big know-all.*

3 · an elephant with a mouse?
   *Big holes in the woodwork.*

4 · an elephant with a kangaroo?
   *Big holes in the outback.*

5 · a bear with a kangaroo?
   *A fur coat with big pockets.*

6 · a kangaroo and a calendar?
   *Leap years.*

7 · a pig and an axe?
*A pork chop.*

8 · a pig and a zebra?
*Striped sausages.*

9 · a porcupine with a skunk?
*A lonely animal.*

10 · an insect with a rabbit?
*Bugs Bunny.*

11 · a shark and a parrot?
*A bird that talks your ears off.*

12 · a cat and a lemon?
*A sourpuss.*

13 · a frog with an ice-cream?
*A lollihop.*

14 · an acorn with a loaf of bread?
*A doughnut.*

15 · a lamp and a sandwich?
*A light lunch.*

16 · an electric blanket and a toaster?
*People who pop out of bed.*

17 · a railway line and a pair of pyjamas?
*A track suit.*

18 · an encyclopaedia and a pair of trousers?
*Smarty-pants.*

19 · chewing gum and a yo-yo?
*Something that comes back if you swallow it.*

20 · the Atlantic with the *Titanic*?
*Half-way.*

# 10 Driving Range

Hit each ball into the correct hole to complete the name of a sport. Then take the first letter from each sport in the first hole, the second letter from each sport in the second hole, and so on, and rearrange them to find the name of a Spaniard who would be a whiz at this game!

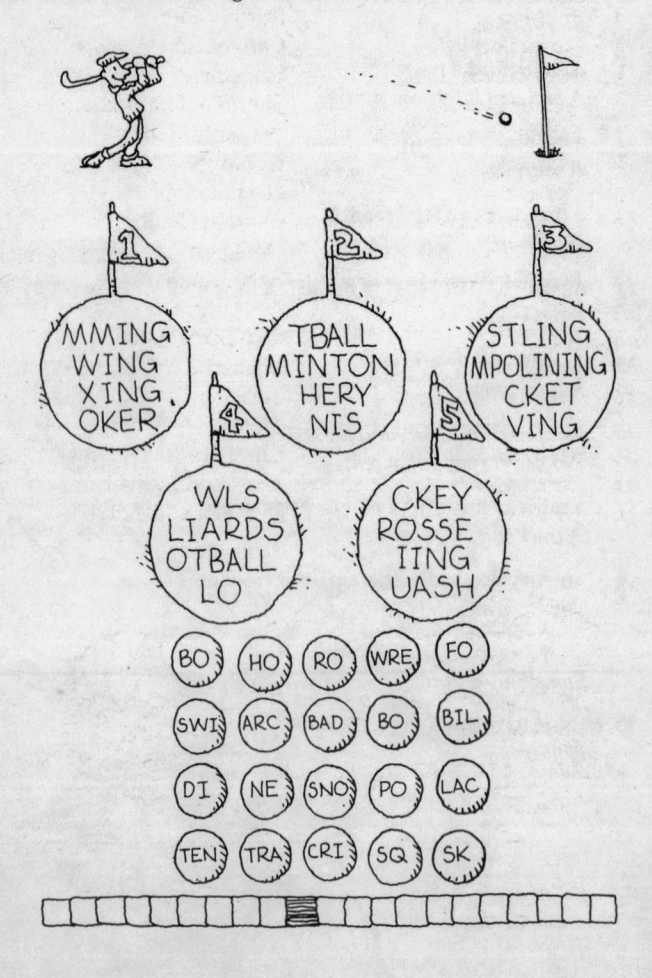

**Hole 1:** MMING, WING, XING, OKER

**Hole 2:** TBALL, MINTON, HERY, NIS

**Hole 3:** STLING, MPOLINING, CKET, VING

**Hole 4:** WLS, LIARDS, OTBALL, LO

**Hole 5:** CKEY, ROSSE, IING, UASH

Balls: BO, HO, RO, WRE, FO, SWI, ARC, BAD, BO, BIL, DI, NE, SNO, PO, LAC, TEN, TRA, CRI, SQ, SK

# 11 The Best of Enemies

Can you match each of the characters with their least favourite person?

| | | |
|---|---|---|
| 1 · | Dennis the Menace | Sylvester |
| 2 · | Robin Hood | Mr Boff |
| 3 · | He-Man | Darth Vader |
| 4 · | James Bond | Catwoman |
| 5 · | Tom Brown | Skeletor |
| 6 · | Arthur Daley | Sheriff of Nottingham |
| 7 · | Biggles | Walter, the softy |
| 8 · | Dorothy | Dr No |
| 9 · | Popeye | Flashman |
| 10 · | Captain Pugwash | Captain Hook |
| 11 · | Peter Pan | Dr Doom |
| 12 · | Luke Skywalker | Shere Khan |
| 13 · | Mowgli | Lex Luthor |
| 14 · | Mr Biff | Cut-Throat Jake |
| 15 · | Jerry | Wicked Witch of the West |
| 16 · | Tweety Pie | Tom |
| 17 · | J. R. Ewing | Bluto |
| 18 · | Spiderman | Cliff Barnes |
| 19 · | Superman | Erich von Stalhein |
| 20 · | Batman | Det. Sgt. Chisholm |

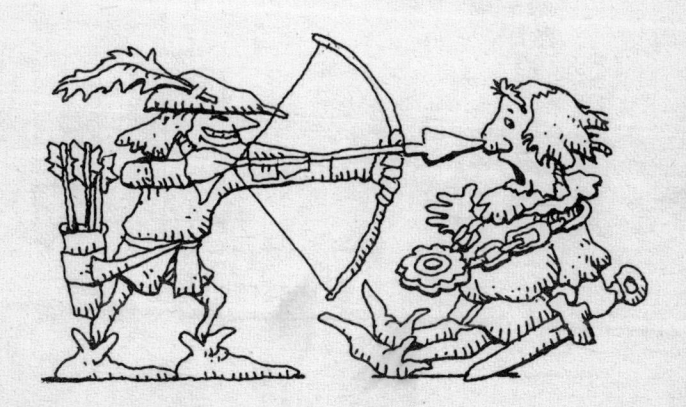

# 12 Ready for Take-off

These flights are all returning to their own capital city, but the flight information board is malfunctioning. Can you fill in the missing letters and find the destinations? Then put the letters in the shaded squares into the grid to find out how and where Concorde is flying.

1. PAN AM
2. EL AL
3. AIR FRANCE
4. QUANTAS
5. SWISSAIR
6. KLM
7. LUFTHANSA
8. AIR LINGUS
9. ICELANDAIR
10. EGYPTAIR
11. AIR CANADA
12. BRITISH AIRWAYS
13. FINNAIR
14. SABENA
15. IBERIA
16. OLYMPIC
17. AIR INDIA
18. ALITALIA
19. JAPAN AIRLINES
20. AEROFLOT

# 13 Men of the World

Each of these groups of men have one thing in common. Do you know what it is?

1. Matthew Corbett, Keith Harris, Rod Hull.
2. Edward Heath, Harold Wilson, James Callaghan.
3. Paul Daniels, the Great Soprendo, Tommy Cooper.
4. Yehudi Menuhin, Stéphane Grappelli, Nigel Kennedy.
5. Patrick Troughton, Colin Baker, Tom Baker.
6. J. F. Kennedy, Martin Luther King, Abraham Lincoln.
7. Steve Davis, Joe Johnson, Hurricane Higgins.
8. Caspar, Melchior, Balthazar.
9. Niki Lauda, James Hunt, Emerson Fittipaldi.
10. Wayne Sleep, Rudolf Nureyev, Mikhail Baryshnikov.
11. John McEnroe, Boris Becker, Ivan Lendl.
12. Erno Rubik, Charles Macintosh, Rudolf Diesel.
13. Gary Player, Tom Watson, Sandy Lyle.
14. Russell Harty, Michael Parkinson, Terry Wogan.
15. Steven Spielberg, George Lucas, John Ford.
16. Jesse James, Ned Kelly, Robin Hood.
17. David Hockney, Pablo Picasso, Vincent van Gogh.
18. David Gower, John Emburey, Ian Botham.
19. Andrew Lloyd Webber, Stephen Sondheim, Leonard Bernstein.
20. Ian Rush, Gary Lineker, Diego Maradona.

# 14 Twenty Questions for High Fliers

Fasten your seat belts! See how fast you can fly through these questions.

**Who flew . . .**
1. to Kensington from Never-Never-Land?
2. too close to the sun and died?
3. Flyer I?
4. messages for the Happy Prince?
5. attached to an umbrella?
6. with a boy in a Raymond Briggs story?
7. the Atlantic in the *Spirit of St Louis*?
8. on a broomstick with a cat called Mog?
9. in the starship *Enterprise*?
10. over Metropolis?

**Which or what . . .**
11. two countries developed Concorde?
12. flew around the world in eighty days?
13. was the R 101?
14. sort of flier was the Super Chicken III?

15 · fictional flier had a friend called Algy?
16 · was the nickname of the German pilot Manfred Freiherr von Richthofen?
17 · Walt Disney elephant could fly?
18 · tree produces 'helicopters'?
19 · sort of aircraft is a 'Flying Bedstead'?
20 · does it mean to travel 'as the crow flies'?

24

# 15 Royal Progress

Take a blue-blooded trip through time with these kings, queens, princes and palaces. Fill in the answers on the grid and then rearrange the letters in the shaded squares to find out what the Queen is doing.

1. The king who owned a legendary round table...
2. ...and the palace in which his famous knights sat round it.
3. The king who sat on the shore ordering the sea not to come in – and got his feet wet.
4. At the Battle of Hastings an arrow hit this king in the eye.
5. The conqueror who started to build the Tower of London.
6. The crusading king who became known as the Lionheart.
7. The ancient Berkshire castle that is still a royal residence.
8. He signed the Magna Carta at Runnymede.

9 · Cardinal Wolsey gave this lavish Thames-side palace to the King . . . (7, 5)
10 · . . . a monarch who had six wives.
11 · The virgin queen whose navy defeated the Spanish Armada.
12 · The king who led the Cavaliers . . . but lost his head at the end . . .
13 · . . . and the palace in front of which he was beheaded.
14 · She became queen at eighteen and reigned for more than sixty years.
15 · Marble Arch once stood outside this palace. Now you may see the Royal Family on the balcony there on special occasions.
16 · Queen Elizabeth II's sister.
17 · The helicopter pilot prince.
18 · Her marriage in 1981 transformed her from a lady to a princess.
19 · Prince William's younger brother.
20 · Sarah Ferguson became duchess of this city when she got married.

# 16 Match the Music

Many singers have turned their talents to acting in films. Can you connect the movie to the star?

1. *Grease*
2. *Labyrinth*
3. *A View to a Kill*
4. *Purple Rain*
5. *Beyond the Thunderdome (Mad Max III)*
6. *Jailhouse Rock*
7. *Summer Holiday*
8. *Give My Regards to Broad Street*
9. *Desperately Seeking Susan*
10. *Tommy*

Prince
Cliff Richard
Roger Daltry
Grace Jones
Elvis Presley

Olivia Newton John
David Bowie
Tina Turner
Paul McCartney
Madonna

**Now see if you can match the song to the show or film from which it came.**

11 · Edelweiss
12 · I Wanna be Like You
13 · Don't Cry for Me, Argentina
14 · Let's Go Fly a Kite
15 · Bright Eyes
16 · Hi Ho, Hi Ho, It's Off to Work We Go
17 · Happy Talk
18 · Memory
19 · Food, Glorious Food!
20 · When the Going Gets Tough (the Tough Get Going)

Cats
South Pacific
Mary Poppins
Evita
The Sound of Music
Watership Down

Oliver!
Romancing the Stone
Jungle Book
Snow White and the Seven Dwarfs

# 17 Tree Word-search

Time to branch out into something different and find twenty British trees hidden in the foliage. They may be written forwards, backwards, diagonally or vertically, and some letters will be used more than once.

| yew | holly | maple | birch | sycamore |
| oak | lime | rowan | cedar | hawthorn |
| ash | pine | larch | willow | chestnut |
| elm | hazel | beech | poplar | hornbeam |

Now use the twenty remaining letters, reading from left to right and top to bottom, to complete this well-known phrase.

MIGHTY _ _ _ _  _ _ _ _  _ _ _ _ _ _ _
_ _ _ _ _ _ _ GROW.

## 18 Back to the Nursery

*Though now you are older,*
*You were once surely told a*
*Number of nursery rhymes.*
*So can you recall*
*The folk in them all*
*From the clues in the following lines?*

**Who...**
1. · was asked to blow his horn?
2. · was christened on Tuesday?
3. · lost something that was empty and had a ribbon round it?
4. · stepped into a puddle in a shower of rain?
5. · wanted to taste a pieman's ware?
6. · was spanked for spoiling her clothes in the cinders?
7. · called for three fiddlers?
8. · marched a lot of men up and down a hill?
9. · picked a peck of pickled pepper?
10. · called his feathered hat Macaroni?
11. · had nothing in her cupboard for her dog?
12. · lived in a little house?
13. · stole some tarts?
14. · had silver buckles on his knee?

15 · fell off a wall and broke into pieces?
16 · washed her hair in turpentine?
17 · had white bread and butter for supper?
18 · lost her holiday shoe?
19 · ran away when the boys came out to play?
20 · couldn't eat fat?

# 19 As Seen on TV

These are all well-known television characters. Can you name the programme in which each one appears? If you can answer them all correctly you are watching far too much television!

1 · Face.
2 · John Ross.
3 · Del boy.
4 · Benny.
5 · Mike Baldwin.
6 · The Fonz.
7 · Mrs Goggins.
8 · Compo.
9 · Mr Spock.
10 · Manuel.
11 · Neil.
12 · Bungle.
13 · Krystle.
14 · Saucy Nancy.
15 · Dolly Skilbeck.
16 · Peggy.
17 · Lofty.
18 · Jacko.
19 · René.
20 · Zammo.

# 20 Criss-cross Words

Solve the clues to fill in the words on the grid. The first and last letters have been given to help you; all diagonal words read from left to right.

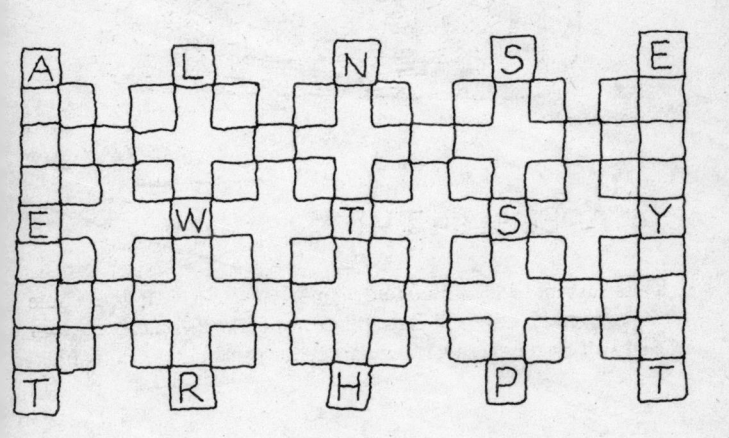

1. A–E: fruit.
2. A–W: old missile.
3. E–L: join up.
4. L–T: extent.
5. W–N: lady.
6. N–S: birds' homes.
7. T–S: trials.
8. S–Y: tale.
9. S–E: coast.
10. E–Y: no contents.
11. E–T: to be.
12. E–R: mistake.
13. T–W: toss.
14. W–H: anger.
15. R–T: cook in oven.
16. T–P: vagrant.
17. H–S: cures.
18. S–T: small fish.
19. P–Y: social gathering.
20. Y–T: boat.

# 21 Crack the Word

One word in the middle of these crackers will complete the first word or phrase and begin the second. See if you can find them all.

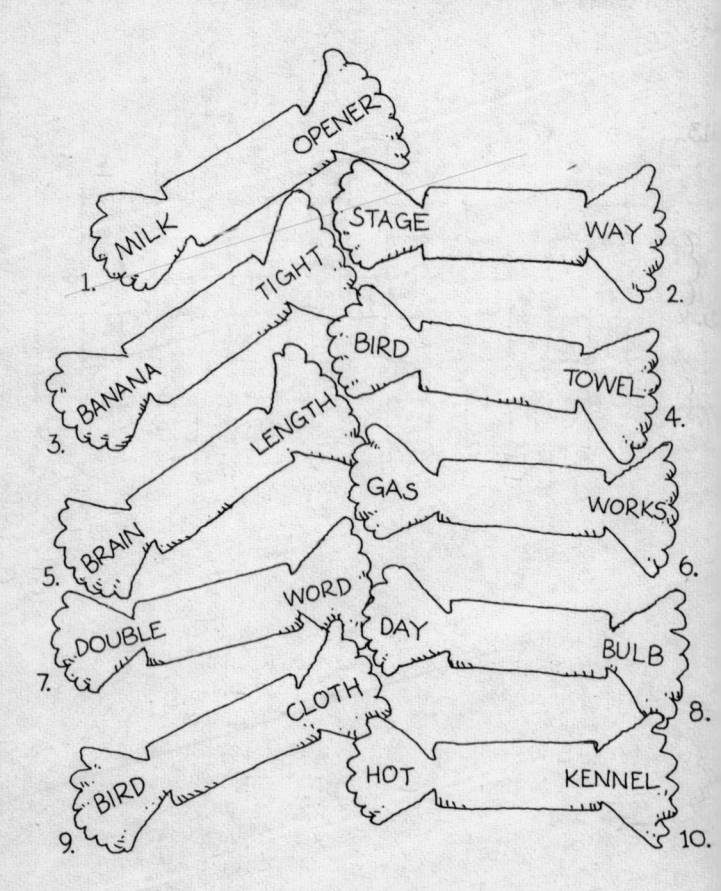

1. MILK — OPENER — STAGE
2. STAGE — ? — WAY
3. BANANA — TIGHT — ...
4. BIRD — ? — TOWEL
5. BRAIN — LENGTH — ...
6. GAS — ? — WORKS
7. DOUBLE — WORD — ...
8. DAY — ? — BULB
9. BIRD — CLOTH — ...
10. HOT — ? — KENNEL

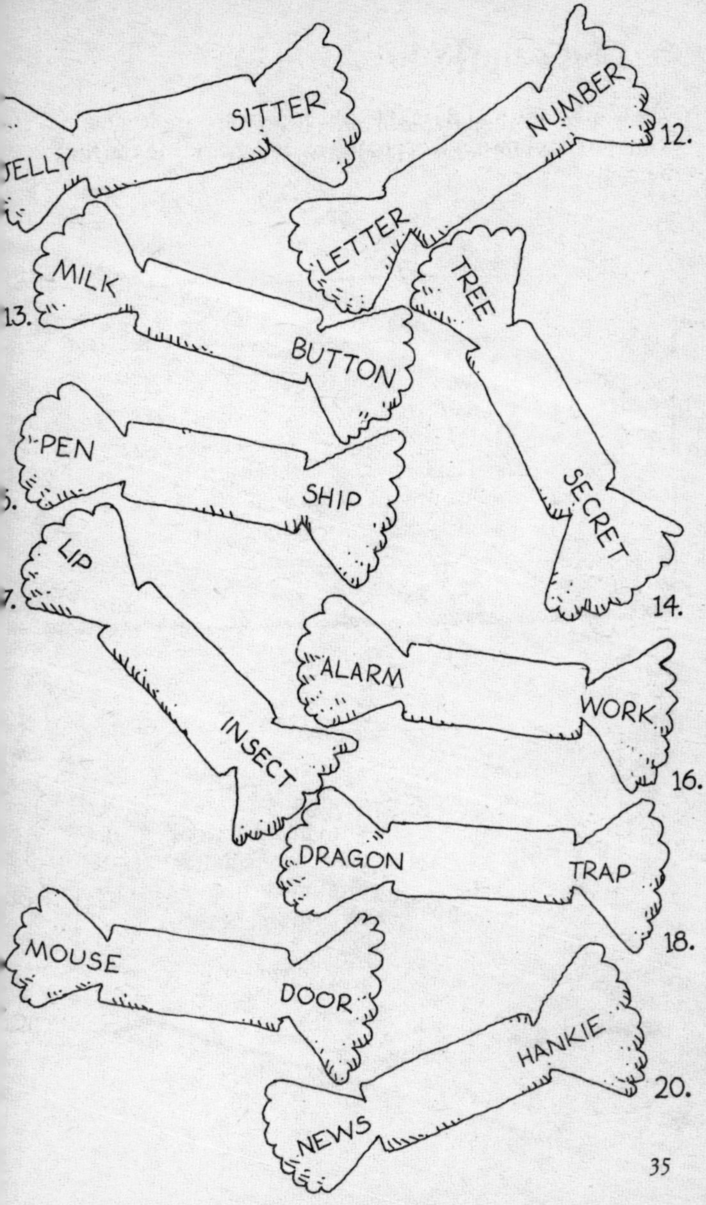
JELLY
SITTER
NUMBER
12.
LETTER
MILK
13.
TREE
BUTTON
PEN
SHIP
SECRET
14.
LIP
ALARM
WORK
16.
INSECT
DRAGON
TRAP
18.
MOUSE
DOOR
HANKIE
20.
NEWS

## 22 Arty-crafty

Are you in the right frame of mind to do this artistic quiz? Simply match the left- and right-hand columns correctly.

**Painters and paintings**
1 · Leonardo da Vinci    The Night Watch
2 · Renoir    Mona Lisa
3 · van Gogh    Guernica
4 · Picasso    Sunflowers
5 · Rembrandt    The Umbrellas

**What is**
6 · *Trompe-l'œil*    wall painting
7 · Fresco    pictures inlaid in wood
8 · Mosaic    an illusion in painting
9 · Tapestry    pictures made from small tiles
10 · Marquetry    pictures in stitches

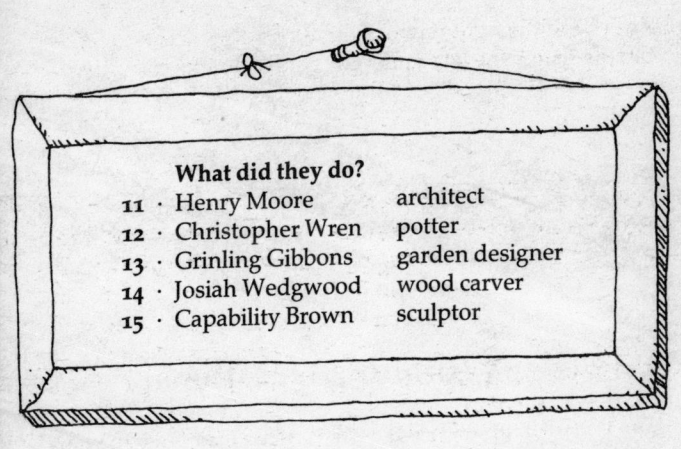

### What did they do?
11. Henry Moore — architect
12. Christopher Wren — potter
13. Grinling Gibbons — garden designer
14. Josiah Wedgwood — wood carver
15. Capability Brown — sculptor

### Who would use?
16. Vellum — printer
17. Gouache — sculptor
18. Slip — artist
19. Chisel — scribe
20. Woodblock — potter

## 23 Twenty Running Questions

Can you keep up with these well-known runners? On your marks, get set, go!

**Who . . .**
1. ran through the town in his nightgown?
2. ran away from a palace when the clock struck twelve?
3. ran up the clock in the nursery rhyme?
4. ran after a farmer's wife and lost their tails?
5. ran a race with a hare and won?
6. ran away with a pig?
7. ran after a rabbit and fell down a hole?
8. ran away from Grimes the chimney-sweep and became a water-baby?
9. ran messages in winged sandals for the Roman gods?
10. ran away from an undertaker and met the Artful Dodger?

**Which or what . . .**
11. vegetable is a runner?
12. was a Bow Street Runner?
13. runs faster – a zebra or a giraffe?
14. name is given to a forty-two-kilometre race?

15 · happens to a runner who makes two false starts in a race?
16 · British runner broke three world records in 1981?
17 · do runners pass to each other in a relay race?
18 · runner ran the first four-minute mile?
19 · famous horse race is run at Epsom in June?
20 · is faster – to run one kilometre in five minutes or five kilometres in one hour?

## 24 Twenty Jumping Questions

Did you know that a flea can jump 130 times its own height? Test your mental agility by leaping through this quiz.

**Which or what . . .**

1 · animal jumped over the moon in the nursery rhyme?
2 · famous Red Indian chief had a father called Jumping Bull?
3 · marsupial can move in leaps of nine metres?
4 · are the three parts of the triple jump in athletics?
5 · was a small step for a man but a giant leap for mankind?
6 · are you supposed to do before you leap?
7 · American stuntman introduced motor-cycle long jumping?
8 · are the poles in the pole vault usually made from?
9 · famous horse race includes a jump called the 'Chair'?
10 · sport has jumps such as the Walley or the Lutz?
11 · is the direction in which one piece in draughts may jump another?
12 · happens in a 'jump off'?
13 · sort of jumping do you associate with Lucinda Green?
14 · sport sends competitors up to six metres into the air?

15 · did nimble and quick Jack jump over in the nursery rhyme?
16 · number of hurdles are there in a 400-metre race?
17 · are jump-leads used for?
18 · sport includes a style of jumping called a Fosbury Flop?
19 · nation enjoys canal jumping as a pastime?
20 · This gymkhana course has been laid out in a special order. Can you put the six fences in the right order?

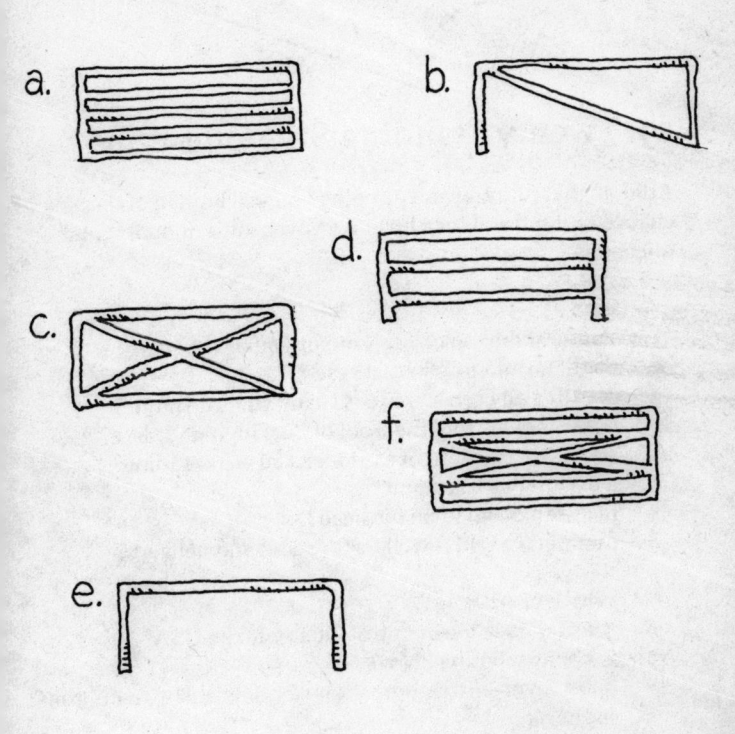

a.

b.

c.

d.

f.

e.

## 25 Twenty Standing Still Questions

After all that running and jumping you will be glad of the chance to stand still for a bit and answer some 'monumental' questions.

**Who . . .**
1. stands at the top of a column in Trafalgar Square?
2. might be told to 'stand at ease'?
3. says 'It's all I can stans, cos I can't stans no more'?
4. never moves from the front of Buckingham Palace?
5. stands on the right of a bridegroom at a wedding?
6. led a famous last stand?
7. incessantly stood on his head?
8. might have told travellers to 'Stand and deliver!'?

**Which or what . . .**
9. country gave the Statue of Liberty to the USA?
10. is a sentry-box used for?
11. sport involves the competitor standing still with his arms in the air?
12. London park has a corner where people can stand up and speak?
13. column stands as a reminder of the Great Fire of London?

14 · statue in Kensington Gardens would you associate with a book?
15 · statue stands at the entrance to Copenhagen Harbour?
16 · memorial stands at Mount Rushmore?

**In which cities would you see these famous structures?**

17.

18.

19.

20.

# 26 My Word!

You know the words – but did you know where they came from?

1 · BADMINTON got its name from the seat of the Dukes of Beaufort at Badminton, where they started shuttling in the 1860s.
2 · BLOOMERS were named after Amelia Bloomer. They were originally Turkish trousers tucked in round the ankles.

3 · BOBBY, a slang word for a policeman, is derived from Sir Robert Peel, the man behind the force.
4 · BUNGALOW got its name from *bangla*, meaning belonging to Bengal. It was originally used as a European's house, usually of one storey.
5 · CANTER was first called the Canterbury pace, as set by pilgrims riding to the shrine of St Thomas à Becket at Canterbury.

6 · CARDIGAN. The garment was named after the seventh Earl of Cardigan, who invented it to keep his men warm in the Crimea.
7 · CIGAR comes from cicada, the Spanish name for a cigar-shaped insect.

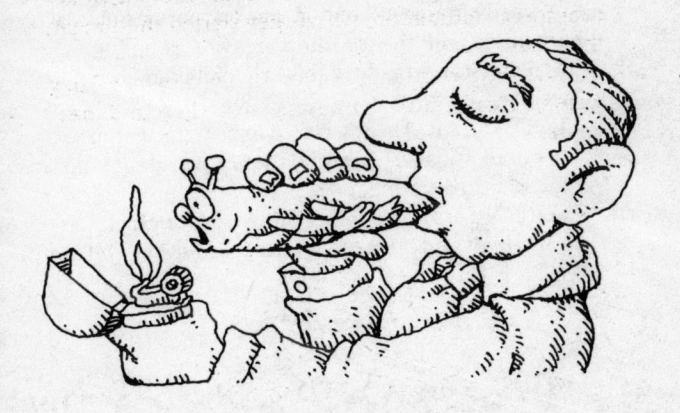

8 · EXCHEQUER is so called because a chequered cloth was once used to make calculations.
9 · GUILLOTINE. Joseph Guillotine, a French doctor, recommended its use to minimize pain in beheading. Ouch!
10 · MAYONNAISE. A sauce that was first made in Port Mahon in Minorca.
11 · PEACH MELBA is named after Dame Nellie Melba, an Australian opera singer who had a sweet tooth.
12 · PULLMAN is named after George M. Pullman of Chicago, designer of well-fitted railway carriages.
13 · RAGLAN. An overcoat with no shoulder seams, first worn by Lord Raglan in the Crimean War.
14 · RUGBY. Rugby football is named after the school Rugby, where it was first played.

15 · SANDWICH – got its name from the Earl of Sandwich. He did not want to stop gambling to eat, so he ordered the waiter to bring him a piece of meat between two slices of bread.
16 · SARDINE. Small fish that is caught off the coast of Sardinia in the Mediterranean.
17 · SOHO. This area of London was once open fields, which resounded with the old hunting cry of 'Soho!'
18 · SUEDE. Gloves made of this originally came from Sweden.
19 · TEDDY BEAR. The toy is said to be named after Theodore Roosevelt (Teddy) the US president who was fond of bear-hunting.
20 · WELLINGTON BOOTS. These were originally a type of riding-boot and are named after the Duke of Wellington.

## 27 Heroes and Heroines

The exploits of these men and women are enough to make us shake in our shoes. Be brave and see if you can match the people to the deeds.

**She...**
1 · took Bonnie Prince Charlie over the sea to Skye.
2 · was the first woman to fly solo to Australia.
3 · was burned at the stake, but was later made a saint.
4 · was a missionary in China and led 100 children to safety.
5 · helped her father to save the survivors of the wrecked *Forfarshire*.
6 · worked to improve conditions in prisons.
7 · was the nurse who became known as the 'Lady with the Lamp'.
8 · led the Iceni in revolt against the Romans.
9 · hid from the Germans in a secret room and kept a diary.
10 · led the suffragettes to get votes for women.

Elizabeth Fry . . . Grace Darling . . . Gladys Aylward . . . Joan of Arc . . . Florence Nightingale . . . Flora Macdonald . . . Amy Johnson . . . Emmeline Pankhurst . . . Anne Frank . . . Boadicea

**He . . .**

11 · built an empire and ruled it wisely.
12 · 'killed him a bear when he was only three' and was himself killed at the Alamo.

13 · is said to have shot an apple from his son's head.
14 · made the first solo flight across the Atlantic.
15 · was a doctor, missionary and explorer in Africa.
16 · defeated the combined fleets of France and Spain at Trafalgar.
17 · campaigned peacefully for black civil rights in America.
18 · funded his African hospitals by giving organ recitals.
19 · led the Arabs against the Turks in the First World War.
20 · was the first man to reach the South Pole.

William Tell . . . Horatio Nelson . . . Albert Schweitzer . . . Davy Crockett . . . Charles Lindbergh . . . Alexander the Great . . . Martin Luther King . . . David Livingstone . . . Thomas E. Lawrence . . . Roald Amundsen

# 28 Twenty Fruit Facts

How much do you know about fruit? Some of the following are true and some false. Can you sort out which is which?

1 · Raisins are dried gooseberries.
2 · Avocado pears are also called alligator pears.
3 · Oranges originally came from China.
4 · Cider is made from raspberries.
5 · There are over 3,000 named varieties of apples.
6 · Honeydew, Galia and Ogen are all kinds of melon.
7 · Nell Gwyn sold lemons.
8 · A prune is a dried plum.
9 · Tomatoes are fruits.
10 · New York is sometimes called the 'Big Apple'.
11 · Perrier water is made from pears.
12 · Pineapples grow on trees.
13 · Williams and Conference are varieties of pear.
14 · Toffee apples grow on the caramel tree.
15 · The first cargo of bananas came to England in 1882.
16 · The blackberry is the rarest fruit in England.
17 · Bananaland is the nickname of Queensland, Australia.
18 · Red wine comes from red grapes.
19 · The Blenheim orange is a kind of apple.
20 · Kirsch is a white brandy made from strawberries.

DOG FOOD
EXCALIBUR
FROBSCOTTLE
WASH WHITE
HONEY
LITTER
EXTRA PACK ELASTOPLAST
TRAIN SET
INVENTIONS
INSURANCE FOR HOUSES
MAGIC BEANS

# BARGAIN MARKET

## 29 Characters in Search of a Bargain

All these story-book characters are in search of a bargain at the market stall. What will they buy?

1. The Mad Hatter.
2. King Arthur.
3. Snow White.
4. The BFG.
5. The Wombles.
6. Mrs Tiggywinkle.
7. Professor Branestawm.
8. The Pied Piper.
9. The Dearlys.
10. Just William.
11. The Three Little Pigs.
12. Jack.
13. Dick Whittington.
14. Paddington Bear.
15. Bluebeard.
16. The Fat Controller.
17. Pooh.
18. Mr Bump.
19. The Railway Children.
20. Fungus the Bogeyman.

## 30 Celebrations!

These clues are all about festivals and celebrations. Fill in the answers on the grid and the shaded letters will tell you something about the bed and who is getting into it.

1 · Festival that gives thanks for good crops of food.
2 · Toss these on Shrove Tuesday.
3 · Jewish Day of Atonement. (3, 6)
4 · Celebrations in America on the fourth of this month.
5 · The day of the Resurrection.
6 · Patron saint of Ireland whose day is 17 March.
7 · Carnival Day in New Orleans, held on 'Fat Tuesday'. (5, 4)
8 · English patron saint said to have fought a dragon.
9 · These are often built on Guy Fawkes night.
10 · Time to make your resolutions for the next twelve months. (3, 4)
11 · You may dance around the maypole today. (3, 3)
12 · Scottish patron saint whose day is 30 November.
13 · The day the angel of death passed over the homes of the Israelites.
14 · Hang out your stocking this evening. (9, 3)
15 · Hindu festival of lights.

16 · Ghosts and ghouls are about tonight.
17 · First visitor after midnight on New Year's Eve. (5, 6)
18 · 26 December: is it a sporting or a packing day? (6, 3)
19 · Scottish new-year festival.
20 · Lovers send anonymous cards on this saint's day.

# 31 Beastly Books

All these animals appear in literature. Can you identify the beast and the book?

**Who had a problem with . . .**
1 · a tar-baby?
2 · the loss of his tail?
3 · his nose, as a result of his curiosity?
4 · an internal clock?
5 · his lack of courage?

**Who travelled . . .**
6 · from Sandleford Warren to Watership Down?
7 · with his wife and puppies from Suffolk to Regent's Park?
8 · from Darkest Peru to a London station?
9 · home across the wilds of Canada?
10 · regularly on the Night Mail?

**Who saved . . .**
11. Faline the fawn from the hunting dogs?
12. Wilbur from the butcher's knife?
13. Mole from freezing in the Wild Wood?
14. Mr Tumnus from a life of stone?
15. his family from Bunce, Bean and Boggis?

**Who belongs to . . .**
16. Meg?
17. Postman Pat?
18. Johnny Briggs?
19. Long John Silver?
20. Deborah Robinson?

## 32 Quick Change

Have you ever wanted to change your name or your appearance? These questions are all connected with some kind of transformation.

**Who or what was transformed . . .**
1. · into six footmen by a fairy godmother?
2. · into a mouse by Puss in Boots?
3. · into the King of the Wild Things?
4. · from a journalist into a superhero?
5. · from being the Worst Witch into a school heroine?
6. · into a swan in a Hans Andersen story?
7. · by Spottyman into a bear with magic powers?
8. · into a pig in *Alice's Adventures in Wonderland*?
9. · into a donkey and sold to a circus?
10. · from Eric into a superhero?

**All these are real people who are better known by other names. Who are they?**
11. · Elaine Bickerstaff had a hit with Barbara Dickson.
12. · David Jones was also known as Ziggy Stardust.
13. · Paul Pond got involved with beating teachers.

14 · Frederick Bulsara joined a regal group.
15 · George O'Dowd joined a club.
16 · Reginald Dwight became a director of Watford football club.
17 · Richard Starkey became a star.
18 · Harry Webb ended up doing *Time*.
19 · Gordon Sumner buzzed around with the Police.
20 · Mary Ciccone desperately looked for Susan.

## 33 Happy Families

Twenty questions about real and fictional relatives.

**Who is or was . . .**
1 · the Duchess of York's mother-in-law?
2 · Fred Flintstone's wife?
3 · Luke Skywalker's sister?
4 · Ryan O'Neal's son-in-law?
5 · Sarah Brightman's husband?
6 · the uncle of Huey, Dewey and Louie?

7 · Bob Geldof's wife?
8 · John Lloyd's wife?
9 · the nephew of Aunt Lucy from Peru?
10 · Nigel Clough's father?
11 · Carol and Mark's mum?
12 · Guinevere's husband?
13 · Catherine of Aragon's second husband?
14 · Michael Douglas's father?
15 · the nephew of Aunt Spiker and Aunt Sponge?
16 · Fungus the Bogeyman's son?
17 · the brother of Groucho, Chico, Gummo and Zeppo?
18 · Elizabeth I's half-sister?
19 · Keith Chegwin's wife?
20 · Viscount Linley's mother?

## 34 For Your Bookshelf

Some light reading for quiet moments!

1 · *In the Jungle* by Lionel Rore.

2 · *Rodeo Riding* by Buck N. Bronco.
3 · *Tummy Rumbles* by Ali Mentary.
4 · *Interpol* by Laura Norder.
5 · *Queen for Twenty-four Hours* by Roy Alday.
6 · *Food Poisoning* by Sam and Ella Jermes.
7 · *The Chocolate Eater* by Kit E. Catte.
8 · *Big Ship Sailing* by Ali Owe.
9 · *Olde Englishe* by Gaye Licke.
10 · *Any Suggestions?* by Ivor Nidear.
11 · *Cheat at Gambling* by Mark D. Card.

12 · *No More Left* by Peter Dout.
13 · *A Soldier's Life* by Reg E. Ment.
14 · *Deep New Snow* by Chris Pennyven.
15 · *Vampires About* by Terry Fide.
16 · *Indecision* by Will E. Wontie.
17 · *Taking the Blame* by Carrie D. Cann.
18 · *No Problems* by P. Surkake.
19 · *What am I Bid?* by N. E. Ophas.
20 · *Italian Food* by Pete Sureeta.

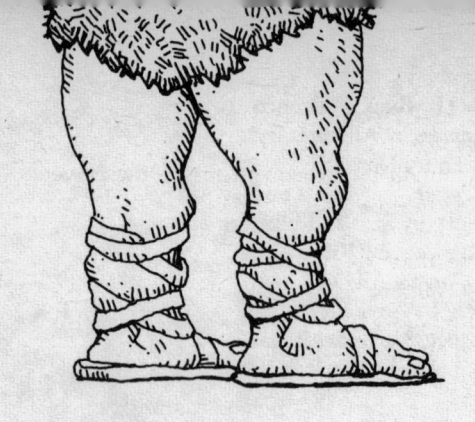

## 35 Think Small

Are you small-minded enough to know who all these 'little' people are?

**Who...**
1. had a plum on his thumb?
2. did Cedric Errol become?
3. was frightened by a spider?
4. was Charles Sherwood Stratton better known as?
5. were the seven dwarfs?
6. lived beneath the floorboards of the 'human beans'?
7. visited her large-toothed grandmother?
8. were the Little Women?
9. cried 'God bless us every one!'?
10. shrank as a result of holding a fan?
11. were the Lilliputians?
12. said 'I think I can – I think I can'?
13. was Robin Hood's tall friend?
14. popped back the maid's nose?
15. were the Munchkins?
16. was told to leave her charges to come home alone?
17. went to live with 'Daddy' Warbucks?
18. froze to death in the snow?
19. were huffed and puffed at by the Big Bad Wolf?
20. lives with Hare and Squirrel?

# 36 Larger than Life

It will help if you think 'big' when you answer these twenty questions.

**Name these 'Bigs'...**
1. A rabbit in *Watership Down*.
2. Noddy's friend.
3. A bell for a famous clock.
4. It sails on the Alley-O.
5. A fun-fair ride that goes round and round.

**Which...**
6. giant stole a magic harp?
7. boy had a nose which grew bigger when he told lies?
8. biblical giant was killed by David?
9. vegetable was so big that it took a dozen people to pull it up?
10. giant was large and sociable?
11. story describes dogs with eyes the size of saucers?
12. character in James Bond films is known for his size and steel dentures?

13 · traveller seemed like a giant to the people of Lilliput?
14 · giant would not allow children to play in his garden?
15 · medicine made a grandmother bigger than a house?
16 · is the largest living land animal?
   a) the African elephant
   b) the hippopotamus
   c) the polar bear.
17 · is the largest living bird?
   a) the bald eagle
   b) the king penguin
   c) the ostrich.
18 · is the largest of all animals?
   a) an Indian elephant
   b) a blue whale
   c) a crocodile.
19 · is the biggest breed of dog?
   a) Alsatian
   b) Labrador
   c) St Bernard.
20 · is the biggest of these dinosaurs?
   a) stegosaurus
   b) brachiosaurus
   c) fabrosaurus.

# 37 Criss-cross Words

Solve the clues and fill in the missing words on the grid. The first and last letters have been given to help you; all diagonal words read from left to right.

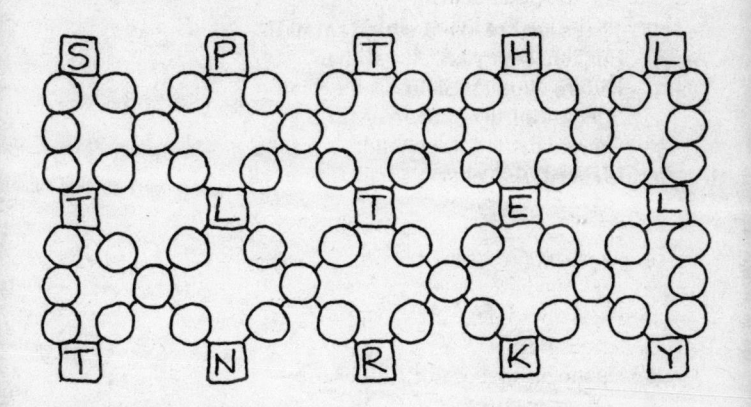

1. S–T: begin.
2. S–L: mar.
3. T–P: unit of soldiers.
4. P–T: put in the ground.
5. L–T: smallest.
6. T–E: temporary cease-fire.
7. T–H: not a lie.
8. H–L: guest house.
9. E–L: praise.
10. L–L: even.
11. T–T: grilled bread!
12. T–N: form of transport.
13. T–L: track.
14. L–R: light beer.
15. N–T: not day.
16. T–K: consider.
17. R–E: elevate.
18. E–Y: foe.
19. K–L: rest on knees.
20. L–Y: tall and thin.

63

# 38 Pet Shop Posers

Did you know that it is illegal to sell a pet to anyone under twelve in Britain? Or that we spend more per year on pet food than we do on baby food? Test your animal expertise and try this quiz.

**These are breeds of which animal?**
1 · English, Peruvian, Abyssinian.
2 · Dutch, Flemish Giant, Californian.
3 · Shetland, Dartmoor, Welsh.
4 · Comet, Fantail, Lionhead.
5 · Mallard, Aylesbury, Khaki Campbell.

**True or False?**
6 · Kittens are blind at birth.
7 · Hares are large rabbits.
8 · Turkeys are very intelligent animals.
9 · Siamese cats have green eyes.
10 · The Queen does not need a dog licence.

**Connect the pet to the food it would enjoy the most.**

11 · Budgerigar    sunflower seeds
12 · Horse         greenflies
13 · Frog          oats
14 · Hamster       a bone
15 · Dog           millet seed

**All these animals have lost their way home. Where should they be?**

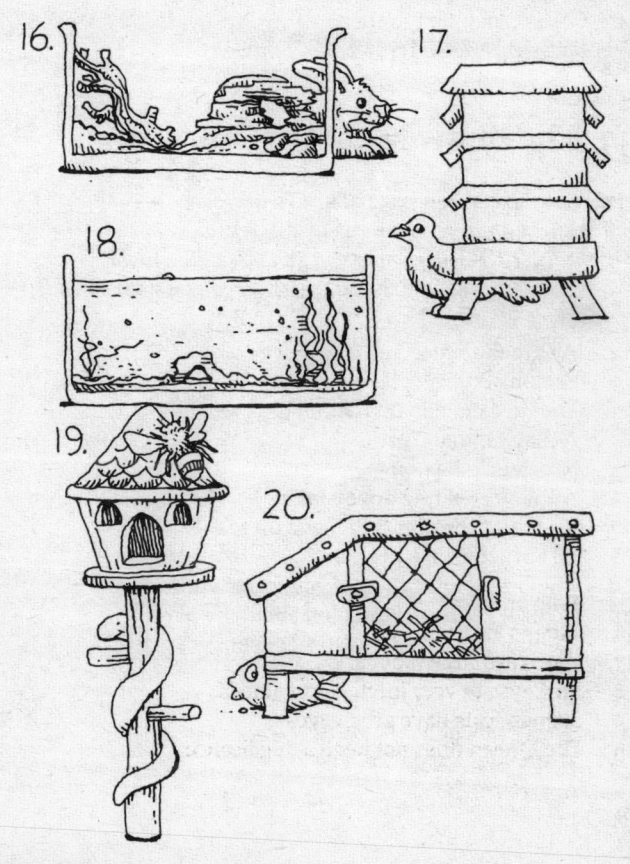

16.

17.

18.

19.

20.

## 39 The Show Must Go On!

*Have your tickets ready and roll up to see the show.*
*Fill in all the answers on the grid you see below.*
*The shaded letters tell you who will give you quite a fright*
*When he sweeps out from the darkness to appear on stage tonight!*

1 · Where the action is.
2 · Famous English playwright.
3 · Theatre began in this country.
4 · A play set to music.
5 · No seats left! (4, 5)
6 · Audience seating downstairs.
7 · Birds and theatres both have these.
8 · List of actors in a play.
9 · You'll get one of these if you forget your words.
10 · Booklet giving information about the play.
11 · Famous American theatrical street.
12 · Scenery gets lifted into here.
13 · A rest between the acts.
14 · These may light your feet!
15 · A story told in dance.

16 · Famous London theatre of Shakespeare's time.
17 · Children's Christmas entertainment.
18 · Buy your tickets here. (3, 6)
19 · The audience may sit round up here.
20 · A performer.

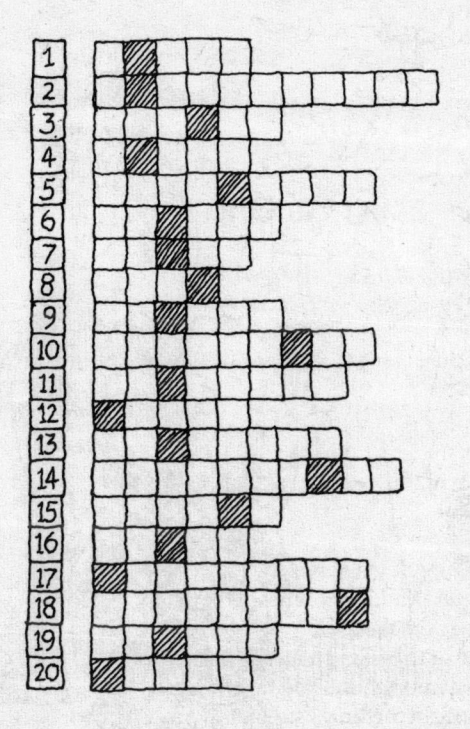

# 40 All Dressed Up

Are you clothes conscious? . . . à la mode? . . . Then here are some questions to which you may ad-dress yourself! All these people in national costume have hung their hats on the hat-stand. Can you tell which country each person is from and to whom each hat belongs?

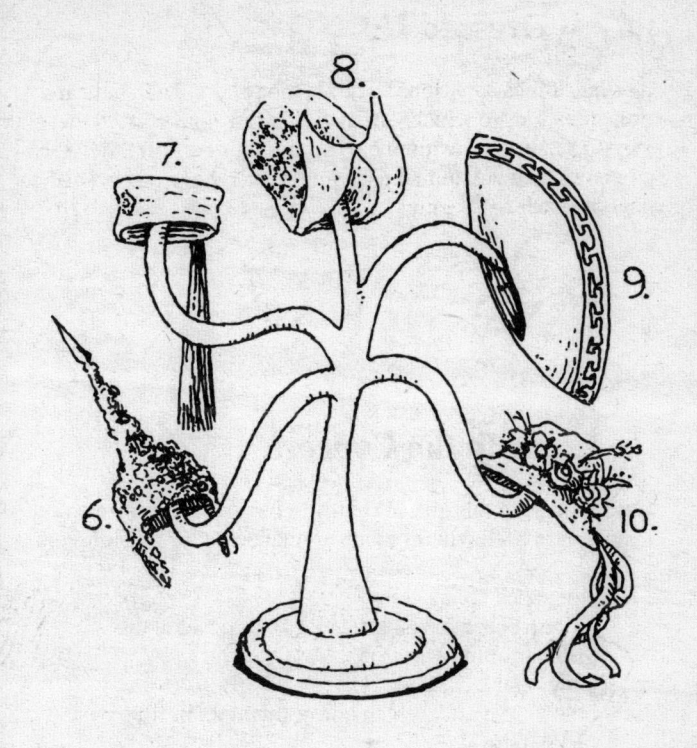

**Who wore . . .**
11. a wolf suit and went to the land of the Wild Things?
12. laughable new clothes?
13. yellow check trousers?
14. a black and white fur coat?
15. a little blue coat with brass buttons?
16. great big waterproof boots?
17. a coat of many colours?
18. red shoes with blue laces?
19. a hat 102 feet wide?
20. magic silver shoes?

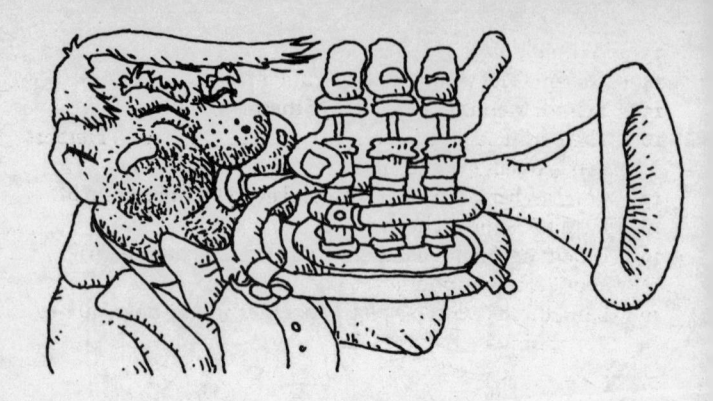

## 41 Come to the Concert

Get tuned in to this quiz. When you have all the answers the last letter of each will reveal an annual event for music lovers.

1 · Not an ice-cream cone!
2 · Johann Sebastian _ _ _ _ , composer of the Brandenburg concertos.
3 · James Galway plays one.
4 · Instrument after which one of the Marx Brothers was nicknamed.
5 · You might play one of these wooden or plastic pipes at school.
6 · You hold this stringed instrument between your knees and bow!
7 · You don't boil water in this kettle.
8 · Geometrical instrument.
9 · Ludwig van _ _ _ _ _ _ _ _ _ , German composer who went deaf before finishing his greatest work.
10 · Large brass instrument.
11 · Early keyboard instrument.
12 · Wooden bars played with a hammer.

13 · Written notes!
14 · The smallest woodwind instrument.
15 · Yehudi Menuhin plays one of these.
16 · The Berlin _ _ _ _ _ _ _ _ _ _ _ _ _ , Herbert von Karajan's orchestra.
17 · You can bang it or shake it – and even tie ribbons on it!
18 · He directs the orchestra.
19 · Wolfgang Amadeus _ _ _ _ _ _ , composer of about fifty symphonies.
20 · Bang these two brass plates together and be heard above everything.

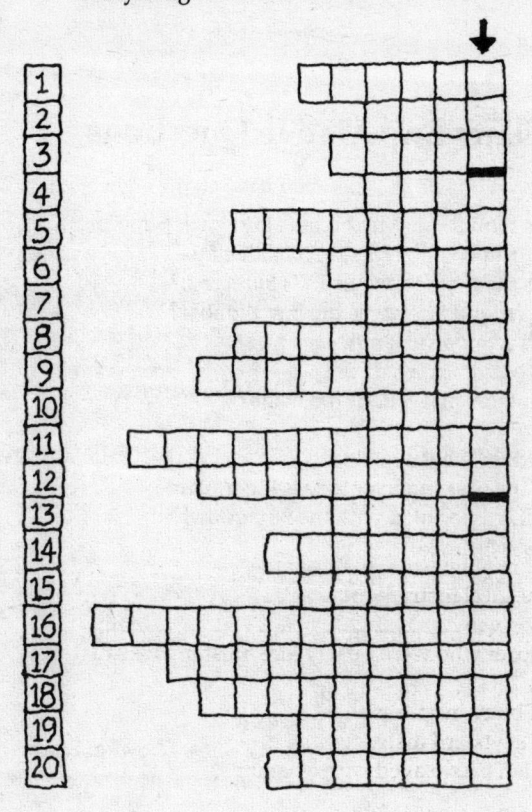

## 42 Twenty Superlative Questions

**Who...**
1. is the tennis star who became known as Superbrat?
2. sang 'Supercalifragilisticexpialidocious'?
3. sings the theme song of TV's *Supergran*?
4. had a friend known as the Boy Wonder?
5. had a wonderful lamp?
6. wrote *Great Expectations*?
7. invented a marvellous medicine?

**Which or what...**
8. was the first supersonic passenger plane?
9. sport is associated with the Superbowl?
10. is a supernova?
11. boxer called himself 'The Greatest'?
12. flag is also known as Old Glory?
13. range of mountains in the USA is known as the Great Divide?
14. country has a Great Wall?
15. is the Great Barrier Reef made of?
16. sort of entertainment was the Greatest Show on Earth?
17. actor starred in the film *Superman*?

**Where . . .**
18 · are the Great Lakes?
19 · was the Great Exhibition held?
20 · might you see the Great Bear?

# 43 Through the Centuries

Have a quick whiz through history with this quiz. Some letters from each answer are there to help you. You start in the first century, AD.

1 · In the first century, which British queen led a revolt?

B _ A _ I _ _ _ _

2 · In the second century, which Roman built a wall in England?

_ A _ R _ A _

3 · In the third century, which civilization invented ink and paper?

_ H _ _ E _ _ _

4 · In the fourth century, which emperor built Constantinople?

_ O _ _ T _ _ T _ _ _

5 · In the fifth century, which saint carried the gospel to Ireland?

_ A _ R _ _ K

6 · In the sixth century, which religious leader was born in Mecca?

_ _ H _ M _ E _

7 · In the seventh century, which famous cathedral was built in Kent?

C _ _ T _ _ B _ _ _

8 · In the eighth century, who came in long ships to invade Britain?

_ I _ _ _ G _

9 · In the ninth century, which king of Wessex was said to burn cakes?

_ _ F _ E _

10 · In the tenth century, which king was known as the Unready?

E _ _ _ L _ _ D

11 · In the eleventh century, which survey was ordered by William I?

_ O _ _ S _ _ Y

74

12 · In the twelfth century, which Japanese fighting force was formed?

S _ M _ R _ _

13 · In the thirteenth century, which grandson of Ghengis became the Great Khan?

K _ _ L _

14 · In the fourteenth century, which disease spread across Europe?

T _ E  B _ _ C _  _ E _ T _

15 · In the fifteenth century, which country was discovered by Vasco da Gama?

_ N _ _ A

16 · In the sixteenth century, who painted the ceiling of the Sistine Chapel?

M _ _ H _ L _ N _ _ L _

17 · In the seventeenth century, which famous Indian monument was built?

T _ _  _ A _ _ L

18 · In the eighteenth century, who sailed to New Zealand in the *Discovery*?

_ A _ _ S  C _ _ K

19 · In the nineteenth century, what made thousands of Americans go west?

_ O _ _

20 · In the twentieth century, which liner sank on its maiden voyage?

_ I _ A _ _ C

# 44 Tourist Attractions

*Twenty monuments, cities, countries and sights*
*You will find if you answer these questions all right.*
*You then take the second letter of each*
*And the twenty-first sight you are certain to reach!*

1. Ancient rings of stones near Salisbury.
2. Famous gorge in Somerset.
3. You could see a monster in this loch.
4. Mumtaz Mahal's white marble memorial at Agra. (3, 5)
5. Scottish village from which the Coronation Chair's Stone of Destiny was taken.
6. A South American capital city designed in the shape of a bow and arrow.
7. The ancient Romans watched great spectacles here.
8. Statue with the head of a pharaoh and body of a lion.
9. Not a good city to be in when Vesuvius erupted in AD 79.
10. The original Olympic Games were held here.
11. Spend a day here with lots of cartoon characters.
12. Queen Victoria's holiday home on the Isle of Wight. (7, 5)
13. Famous cathedral on the Île de la Cité in Paris. (5, 4)
14. Welsh border dike named after a king. (5, 4).
15. Wall in Jerusalem where people gather to pray. (7, 4).
16. Island kingdom said to be under the sea.
17. The longest wall in the world is in this country.
18. St _ _ _ _ _ 's Basilica, a large church in Rome, named after the saint whose bones rest beneath it.

19 · Palace in Crete where the Minotaur is said to have been kept.
20 · The city that started as Byzantium, changed to Constantinople, and now has another name.

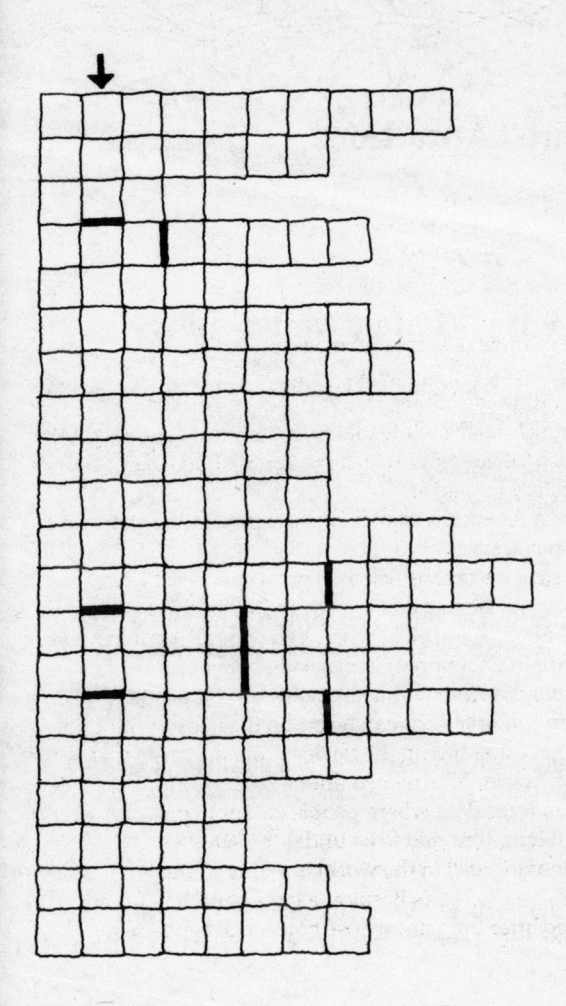

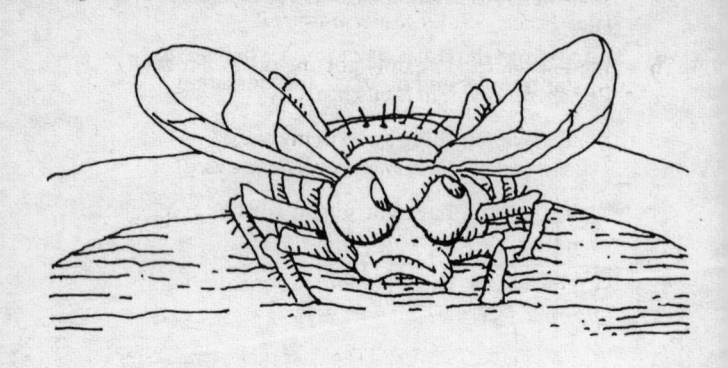

## 45 Twenty 'Waiter, waiter' Jokes

After reading this lot you may feel that you never want to eat in a restaurant again!

1 · 'Waiter, waiter, why does my soup have a fly in it?'
    *'What do you expect for 50p? A chicken?'*

2 · 'Waiter, waiter, do you have frogs' legs?'
    *'No, sir. I always walk like this.'*

3 · 'Waiter, waiter, there's no chicken in my chicken pie.'
    *'Well, you won't find a cat in a tin of cat food either.'*

4 · 'Waiter, waiter, can I have a spoon for my soup?'
    *'Sorry, sir, I can't change orders.'*

5 · 'Waiter, waiter, what's this fly doing in my soup?'
    *'Looks like backstroke to me, sir.'*

6 · 'Waiter, waiter, there's a frog in my soup.'
    *'Oh good. Perhaps he's eaten the fly.'*

7 · 'Waiter, waiter, I'd like a dinosaur sandwich.'
    *'Sorry, sir. We've run out of bread.'*

6 · 'Waiter, waiter, how long will my hot dog be?'
'I don't know, sir. I'll go and measure it.'

9 · 'Waiter, waiter, I've only got one piece of meat.'
'Perhaps Sir could cut it into two.'

10 · 'Waiter, waiter, there's 10p in my soup.'
'The chef thought the change would do you good.'

11 · 'Waiter, waiter, have you got any dishes going cheap?'
'Oh no, sir. We cook all our chickens first.'

12 · 'Waiter, waiter, there's a twig in my soup.'
'I'll go and fetch the branch manager.'

13 · 'Waiter, waiter, how did the chef make the pasta?'
'By using his noodle.'

14 · 'Waiter, waiter, there's a dead fly in my soup.'
'Oh dear, the soup must have been too hot.'

15 · 'Waiter, waiter, I asked for a meat salad.'
'Don't worry. There's bound to be a caterpillar in the lettuce.'

**16** · 'Waiter, waiter, do you serve children?'
'*No, sir. They don't seem to like being cooked.*'

**17** · 'Waiter, waiter, this food is half cold.'
'*Well, you'd better eat the other half quickly then.*'

**18** · 'Waiter, waiter, what is the charge per head?'
'*£5, sir, but you can have an ear for 50p.*'

**19** · 'Waiter, waiter, what is this soup called?'
'*I don't know, sir, but the fly is called Bert.*'

**20** · 'Waiter, waiter, why is there no soup on the menu?'
'*I'm sorry, madam, I've just wiped it off.*'

# 46 Something Fishy

When you see things on the shore are you sure of what you see? Which of these seaside facts are true . . . and which are false?

1 · Sea anemones are animals.
2 · Spring tides occur in springtime.
3 · Barnacles stand on their heads.
4 · Seaweeds have no roots.
5 · Limpets return to the same place after looking for food.
6 · Breadcrumb sponges thrive on picnic leftovers.
7 · An alarmed sea cucumber can discard its interior organs.
8 · Slipper limpets change sex as they age.
9 · Grey seals live in rookeries.
10 · A mermaid's purse is the empty egg-case of the skate, ray and dogfish.
11 · Lobsters are red.
12 · A dog whelk is a carnivore.
13 · Tides are the result of the pulls of gravity of the sun and moon.
14 · Crabs moult their shells.
15 · Starfish can shed their arms.
16 · An eel is a water snake.
17 · Razor shells dig with their feet.
18 · Terns nest on the ground.
19 · Sea slugs are very ugly creatures.
20 · A frightened octopus may squirt out 'ink'.

# 47 Oddities

In each of the lists that follow there is an odd man out. Which is it?

1 · Lens, tripod, amplifier, negative.
2 · Topaz, glass, amethyst, garnet.
3 · Demerara, Basmati, granulated, castor.
4 · Metre, litre, gallon, kilogram.
5 · Morse, braille, semaphore, radar.
6 · Humber, suspension, cantilever, arch.
7 · Volkswagen, Audi, Mercedes, Renault.
8 · Koala, duck-billed platypus, wallaby, kangaroo.
9 · Snail, slug, crab, mussel.
10 · Saturn, Apollo, Jupiter, Pluto.
11 · Emulsion, blotting, litmus, tissue.
12 · Neon, oxygen, helium, iron.
13 · Garibaldi, Nice, Bourbon, Madeira.
14 · Kaleidoscope, stethoscope, microscope, telescope.
15 · Spa, spring, lemonade, mineral.
16 · 27, 18, 16, 81.
17 · Diamond, silver, gold, platinum.
18 · Royal Scot, Mallard, Jumbo, Rocket.
19 · RAM, BASIC, ROM, EEC.
20 · Butterfly, earthworm, mosquito, housefly.

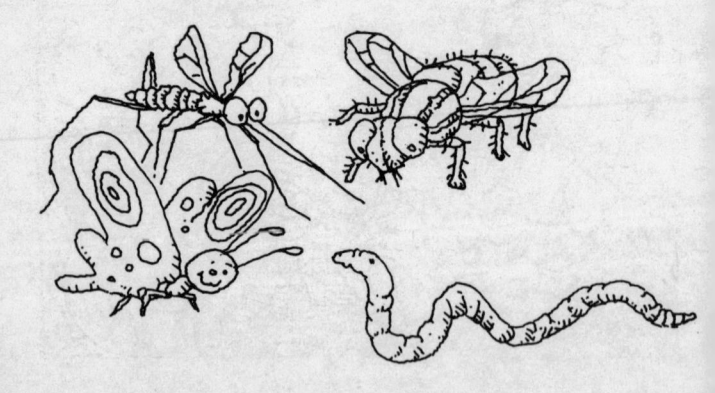

# 48 Musical Beasts

All the songs or singers in this 'beastly' quiz are connected in some way with creatures. What are they?

1. They're having a picnic in the woods.
2. They enjoy mud for cooling the blood.
3. She said goodbye to the circus.
4. Rupert watched them sing.
5. He frolicked in the autumn mist.
6. Elton John rocked with one.
7. He had a red nose.
8. Boy George's lizard.
9. Tiny Adam?
10. He lives in a hole.
11. The bare necessities of life are all he needs.
12. Four human creepy-crawlies.
13. It goes pop.
14. They fought for the crown.
15. Bob Geldof's rodents.
16. Their food costs tuppence a bag.
17. It wandered up and down stairs.
18. See you later!
19. They lived in a windmill in Old Amsterdam.
20. That unpriced waggerly-tailed animal in the window.

# 49 Search Party

Study the scene studiously seeking a score of objects starting with 's'. See how speedily you can spot them!

## 50 Don't Vegetate!

Answer these questions and see if you really know your onions!

**Which or what . . .**
1. did Jack swap his cow for?
2. has 'eyes' but can't see?
3. might make you cry?
4. is a cauliflower ear?
5. is 'spilling the beans'?
6. is also known as egg-plant?
7. is a potato-bogle?
8. dolls come named and ready to adopt?
9. is cabbage to a tailor?
10. is the national emblem of Wales?
11. is sauerkraut?
12. spoiled the Princess's sleep?
13. is said to make you see better in the dark?
14. made the Flopsy Bunnies fall asleep when they ate too much of it?
15. is especially associated with Hallowe'en?

16 · makes Popeye strong?
17 · is an edible thistle?
18 · is bubble and squeak?
19 · vegetable may be found on a £1 coin?
20 · is hotter than its name suggests?

## 51 Dining Out

A banquet has been arranged for some sporting personalities. The chef thought that it would be a good idea to serve each guest with a dish from their own country. Can you work out which item on the menu would be offered to each sportsman?

**Guests**

1 · Kenny Dalglish.
2 · Hugo Sanchez.
3 · Ian Botham.
4 · Chris Evert.
5 · Boris Becker.
6 · Pat Jennings.
7 · Imran Khan.
8 · Paulo Rossi.
9 · Severiano Ballesteros.
10 · Alain Prost.

86

## Menu

Lasagne
Samosas
Quiche Lorraine
Sauerkraut
Roast beef

Paella
Irish stew
Pumpkin pie
Chilli con carne
Haggis

Some literary guests are also going to enjoy their favourite food. Try to match these diners to the correct dinner.

### Guests
11 · Little Miss Muffet.
12 · The Owl and the Pussycat.
13 · Popeye.
14 · The Knave of Hearts.
15 · Little Jack Horner.
16 · Tigger.
17 · Dr Who.
18 · Jeremy Fisher.
19 · Charlie Buckett.
20 · The BFG.

### Menu

Curds and whey
Jelly babies
Extract of malt
Plum pudding
Snozzcumbers and frobscottle

Spinach surprise
Roasted grasshoppers
Jam tarts
Slices of quince
Fudge Mallow Delight

# 52 All in the Game

Twenty questions about games that are played indoors.

**In which game might you . . .**
1. flip a wink?
2. collect relations?
3. hit a jack?
4. knock down pins?
5. call out 'House!'?
6. have a Royal Flush?
7. play with dragons and winds?
8. go down reptiles and climb up rungs?

**In the game of . . .**
9. solitaire, how many players are there?
10. backgammon, what is a blot?
11. dominoes, which piece has the most dots?
12. draughts, do you play on the white or the black squares?
13. snooker, what colour is the cue ball?
14. darts, what is the highest possible score in one turn?

# These pieces have all fallen out of popular games. To which games do they belong?

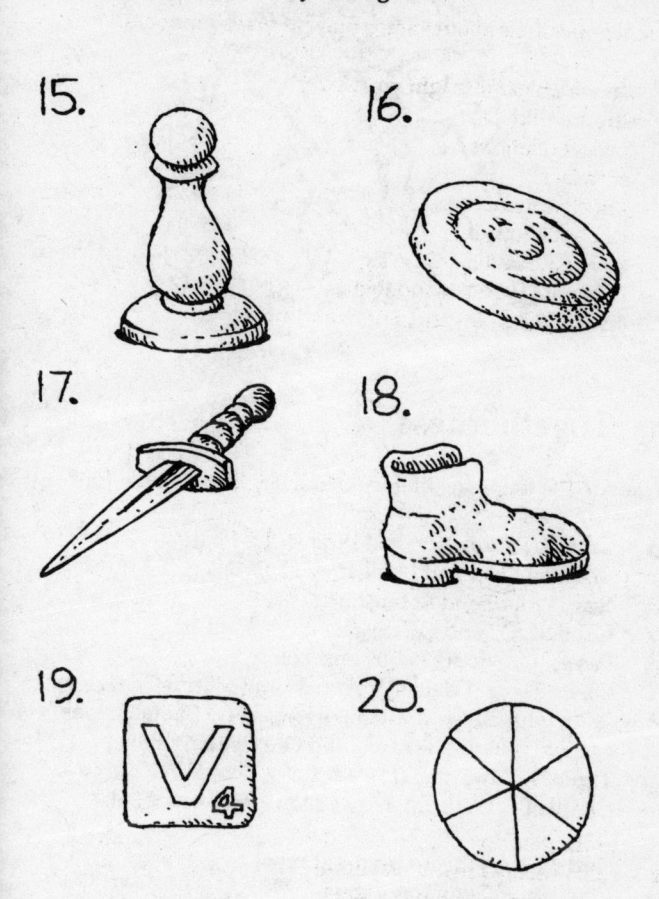

**15.**

**16.**

**17.**

**18.**

**19.**

**20.**

## 53 Togetherness

What do the following literary characters have in common?

1. Rupert, Paddington and Winnie-the-Pooh?
2. Roberta, Peter and Phyllis?
3. Sam, Wilbur and Robinson?
4. Gandalf, Oz and Catweazle?
5. Lassie, Greyfriars Bobby and Tramp?
6. Oliver Twist, David Copperfield and Martin Chuzzlewit?
7. Long John Silver, Captain Pugwash and Captain Hook?
8. Macavity, Skimbleshanks and Old Deuteronomy?
9. Thomas, Edward and Henry?
10. Charlie Buckett, Augustus Gloop and Verruca Salt?

**And who are these famous groups?**
11. John, Paul, George and Ringo
12. Holly, Paul, Mark, Brian and Peter.
13. Freddie, Brian, John and Roger.
14. Morten, Mags and Pal.
15. Siobhan, Keren and Sarah.
16. Stedman, Doris, Lorraine, Delroy and Denise.

17 · Tom and Allanah.
18 · Simon, John, Andy, Roger and Nick.
19 · Agnetha, Anna-Frid, Bjorn and Benny.
20 · Annie and Dave.

## 54 Find the Number

The answers to these clues are all numbers from one to twenty. No number is used more than once. You may find the grid useful for sorting them out.

1 · Days of Lady Jane Grey's reign.
2 · Sides of a triangle.
3 · Age at which Nelson went to sea.
4 · Members of a Rugby Union side.
5 · Highest number on a dartboard.
6 · Riders on a tandem.
7 · Members of a football team.
8 · Wives of Henry VIII.
9 · Age at which Victoria became queen.
10 · The deadly sins.
11 · Fastest formula for a racing car.
12 · Chambers in a cow's stomach.
13 · Goals in the 1986 World Cup final.
14 · Reindeer pulling St Nicholas's sledge.
15 · Official residence of the British prime minister.
16 · Age at which you can leave school in Britain.
17 · Number of lamps in the Statue of Liberty's torch.
18 · Triskaidekaphobia is fear of this number.
19 · Age at which you can hold a pilot's licence.
20 · Age at which Nigel Short became an international chess master.

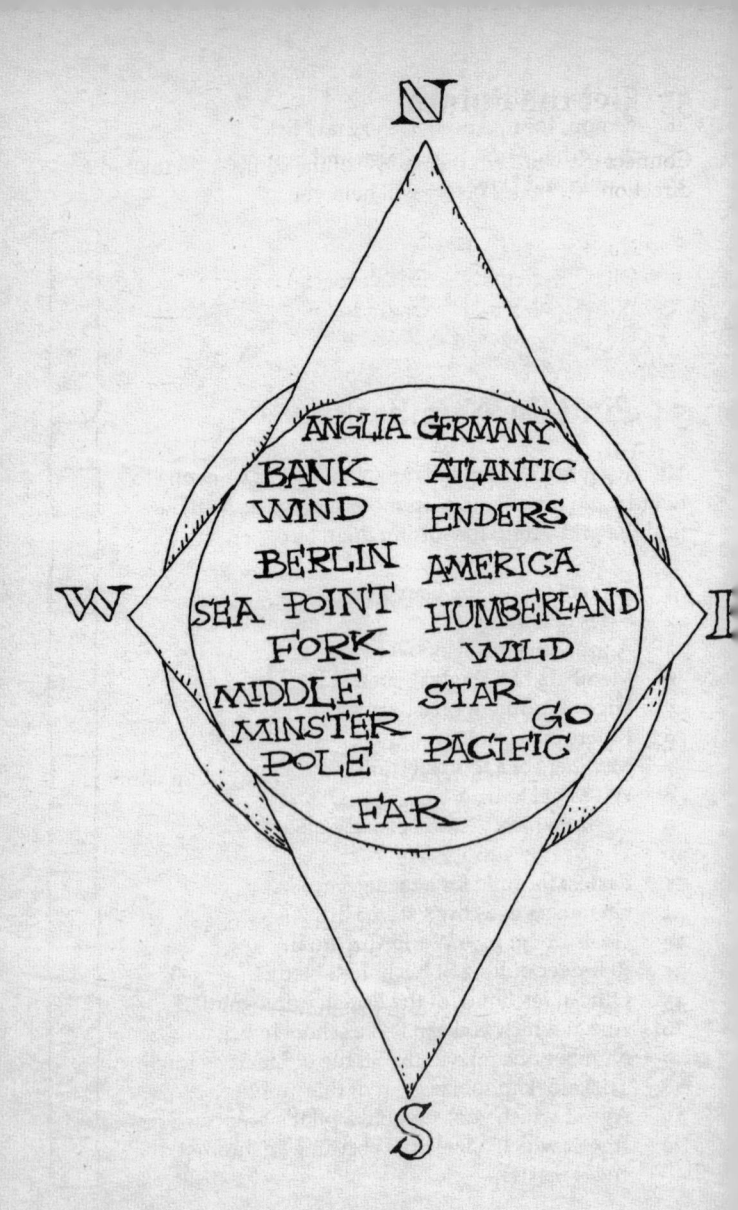

```
        N

   ANGLIA GERMANY
   BANK   ATLANTIC
   WIND   ENDERS
   BERLIN AMERICA
W  SEA POINT HUMBERLAND  E
   FORK   WILD
   MIDDLE STAR
   MINSTER    GO
   POLE   PACIFIC
        FAR

        S
```

# 55 Get the Point?

Connect the words in the middle of the compass to the right direction. The clues below will help you.

### North
1. Oil is found in these British coastal waters.
2. When it blows snow might follow.
3. Otherwise known as Polaris.
4. In the Arctic region.
5. Hadrian's wall is here.

### East
6. A popular soap opera.
7. Suffolk and Norfolk.
8. An area that produces forty per cent of the world's oil.
9. Capital of the German Democratic Republic.
10. Countries of East and South-east Asia.

### South
11. A Rodgers and Hammerstein musical.
12. The ranch home of the Ewings.
13. The Falkland Islands are here.
14. Continent that is home to the 1986 World Cup winners.
15. TV show hosted by Melvyn Bragg.

### West
16. A two-man pop group.
17. Cowboys and Indians lived here.
18. The home of the British Parliament.
19. A US military academy.
20. The capital of this country is Bonn.

## 56 Twenty Questions from Outer Space

You can find your way out of the Black Hole with the help of these clues. The last letter of each answer will begin the next word. The first letter of each word is shown to help you along. Ready for blast off? 10, 9, 8 . . .

1. Space traveller.
2. Instrument used by star gazers.
3. Our planet.
4. He has a comet named after him.
5. 365 earth days.
6. They launch spacecraft.
7. Bodies that orbit a planet.
8. American space laboratory.
9. The first aerial voyages were made in these.
10. Russian spacecraft.
11. Astrologers study the _ _ _ _ _ _ _ .
12. Group of stars.
13. He discovered the laws of gravity.
14. It makes up seventy-eight per cent of the earth's atmosphere.

15 · We can see the stars at this time.
16 · The first woman in space – Valentina
   _ _ _ _ _ _ _ _ _ _ .
17 · _ _ _ _ _ _ 11 took the first men to the moon.
18 · The path taken by a spacecraft.
19 · Constellation and sign of the Zodiac.
20 · What this quiz is about!

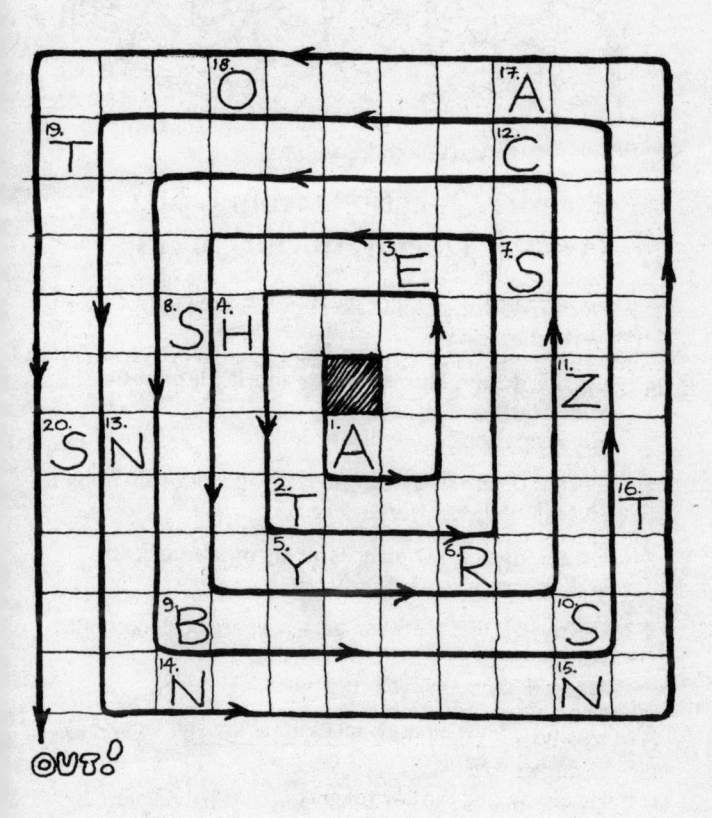

## 57 Twenty 'Doctor, doctor' Jokes

1. 'Doctor, doctor, no one takes any notice of me.'
   *'Next patient please.'*

2. 'Doctor, doctor, I think that my wife is a little potty.'
   *'Why is that?'*
   'She keeps lying under the bed.'

3. 'Doctor, doctor, why are you walking around on tiptoe?'
   *'I don't want to wake the sleeping pills.'*

4. 'Doctor, doctor, my piano is giving me a sore head.'
   *'Well, you must stop playing it by ear.'*

5. 'Doctor, doctor, these contact lenses are no good at all.'
   *'Why is that?'*
   'I can't fit them on over my glasses.'

6. 'Doctor, doctor, nobody takes me seriously.'
   *'You must be joking.'*

7. 'Doctor, doctor, I think I'm a mouse. What do you suggest?'
   *'You had better get rid of your cat.'*

8 · 'Doctor, doctor, I think I'm a bee.'
   *'Buzz off.'*

9 · 'Doctor, doctor, I keep thinking I'm a piano.'
   *'Come back when you are out of tune.'*

10 · 'Doctor, doctor, I think I'm Ian Botham.'
    *'How's that?'*
    'Oh, you have the same problem?'

11 · 'Doctor, doctor, what's the best thing for a bald head?'
    *'Hair.'*

12 · 'Doctor, doctor, what have you got for flat feet?'
    *'Try this foot pump.'*

13 · 'Doctor, doctor, I keep thinking I'm a meat pie.'
    *'What's got into you?'*
    'Steak and kidney mostly.'

14 · 'Doctor, doctor, I think I'm an ice lolly.'
    *'Well, I suggest you stay cool.'*

15 · 'Doctor, doctor, are carrots good for the eyes?'
    *'Have you ever seen a rabbit wearing spectacles?'*

**16** · 'Doctor, doctor, I can't tell the truth.'
'*Would you feel better lying on the couch?*'

**17** · 'Doctor, doctor, I think that I'm a dustbin.'
'*What a lot of rubbish!*'

**18** · 'Doctor, doctor, I keep seeing blue pigs.'
'*Have you seen a psychiatrist?*'
'No, only blue pigs.'

**19** · 'Doctor, doctor, can you help me out?'
'*Of course. The door is over there.*'

**20** · 'Doctor, doctor, my teeth keep falling out. Can you give me anything to keep them in?'
'*How about a paper bag?*'

## 58 Headline News

Read all about it! Can you imagine how newspapers would have announced some famous events? These made-up headlines have real dates to put you on the right track.

1 · 14 October 1066. One in the Eye for Brave Harold.
2 · 15 June 1215. King John Seals It Up.
3 · 19 July 1553. All Over for Nine-days Wonder.
4 · 8 February 1587. Queen's Cousin in Execution Drama.
5 · 29 July 1588. Spanish Fleet in Deep Water.
6 · 5 November 1605. Timely Discovery in the House of Commons.
7 · 6 September 1620. Pilgrims' Progress to America.
8 · 30 January 1649. King Gets the Chop.
9 · 2 September 1666. Bright Spark in Pudding Lane Sets Town Ablaze.
10 · 7 April 1739. Highwayman Makes Final Appearance.
11 · 16 December 1773. Rumpus at New England Harbour.
12 · 28 April 1789. Crew up in Arms on Royal Navy Ship.
13 · 30 April 1789. New Top Office for America.
14 · 18 January 1815. Belgian Defeat for Napoleon.
15 · 1 May 1851. Big Show at the Crystal Palace in Hyde Park.
16 · 10 November 1871. Journalist and Missionary Meet at Last.

- 17 · 18 January 1912. Disappointment at the South Pole.
- 18 · 29 May 1953. Hillary on Top of the World.
- 19 · 22 November 1963. Shooting at Dallas Shakes the World.
- 20 · 20 July 1969. Armstrong Puts his Best Foot Forward.

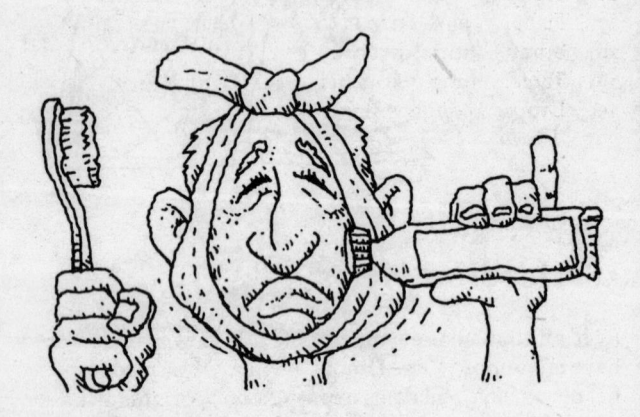

## 59 Up Front

A single word placed in front of each word in the group of three will create three new words or phrases. See if you can find the missing link.

1 · Cake, finger, paste.
2 · Bin, winner, roll.
3 · Éclair, nose, apple.
4 · Cream, age, cube.
5 · Brush, paste, ache.
6 · Fall, works, cress.
7 · Tart, powder, pie.
8 · Mouth, kick, keeper.
9 · Cuff, bag, book.

10 · Worm, shelf, token.
11 · Flap, nap, fish.
12 · Lights, path, prints.
13 · Pot, show, bed.
14 · Castle, paper, pit.
15 · Bus, leaver, book.
16 · Weight, bulb, year.
17 · Fisher, pin, size.
18 · Spray, trap, over.
19 · Table, song, watcher.
20 · Drop, plough, flake.

# 60 A Quiz to Make You Tremble

Throughout history people have been frightening themselves by creating strange creatures with terrifying powers. Test your knowledge of monsters by answering these questions.

1 · Cerberus the dog guarded the gates of hell. How many heads did he have?

2 · King Kong first appeared in a film in 1933. How was he killed?
   a) by falling off the Empire State Building
   b) by eating too much
   c) by falling into the sea.
3 · The job of the Cyclops was to make thunderbolts. They had one eye. Where was it?
4 · Grendel lived in the marshes and ate warriors for dinner. His take-away suppers ended when he was killed by
   a) Odysseus
   b) Sir Lancelot
   c) Beowulf.
5 · The Minotaur also liked to eat humans. Theseus killed him and claimed his reward. Was it
   a) a horse
   b) the king's daughter
   c) a new sword.
6 · Medusa was so ugly that anyone who looked at her was turned to
   a) jelly
   b) glass
   c) stone.
7 · Most dragons are shown as fire-breathing monsters. The Chinese Dragon, however, is regarded as
   a) a symbol of good luck
   b) a god
   c) a bodyguard.
8 · How did the Kraken cause ships to sink?
9 · Frankenstein was the fictional name of a man who made a monster. What was the monster called?
10 · Sasquatch means hairy giant. What do they call him in North America?
   a) Bigfoot
   b) the BFG
   c) Grizzly.
11 · What did the Griffin guard?
   a) a cave
   b) a nest of gold
   c) a royal palace.

12 · In the film *Jaws*, what was the man-eating shark made from?
   a) a dead shark
   b) a waxwork
   c) several mechanical models.

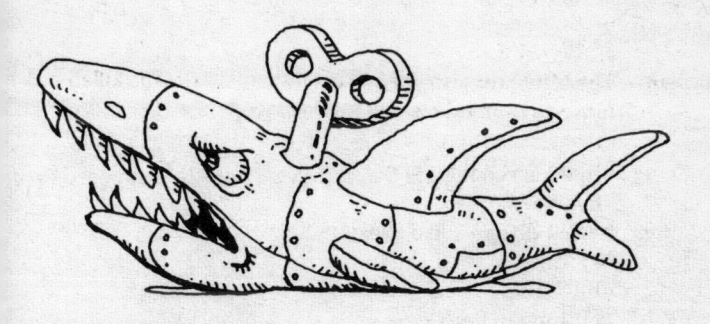

13 · The Chimera had a goat's body and a dragon's tail. What was his head?
14 · Vampires were supposed to be the ghosts of criminals. What did they like to get their teeth into?
15 · More horror films have been made about Dracula than any other vampire. When was he created?
   a) 1944
   b) 1912
   c) 1897.
16 · A werewolf is a man who becomes a wolf at night. What is the only thing that can kill him?
   a) a bow and arrow
   b) a wooden stake
   c) a silver bullet.

17 · In which country is the Loch Ness monster supposed to live?
18 · What do ogres like to eat?
   a) mice
   b) plants
   c) human flesh.
19 · When did man first realize that dinosaurs once existed?
   a) in the nineteenth century
   b) in the sixteenth century
   c) in the twelfth century.
20 · The roc was a huge bird, shaped like an eagle. In which story does he appear?
   a) Aladdin
   b) Sindbad the Sailor
   c) Cinderella.

All the names mentioned in the questions are hidden inside the mummy. Sometimes a letter is used twice. When you have found them all take out the twenty solid letters and create the name of yet another monster.

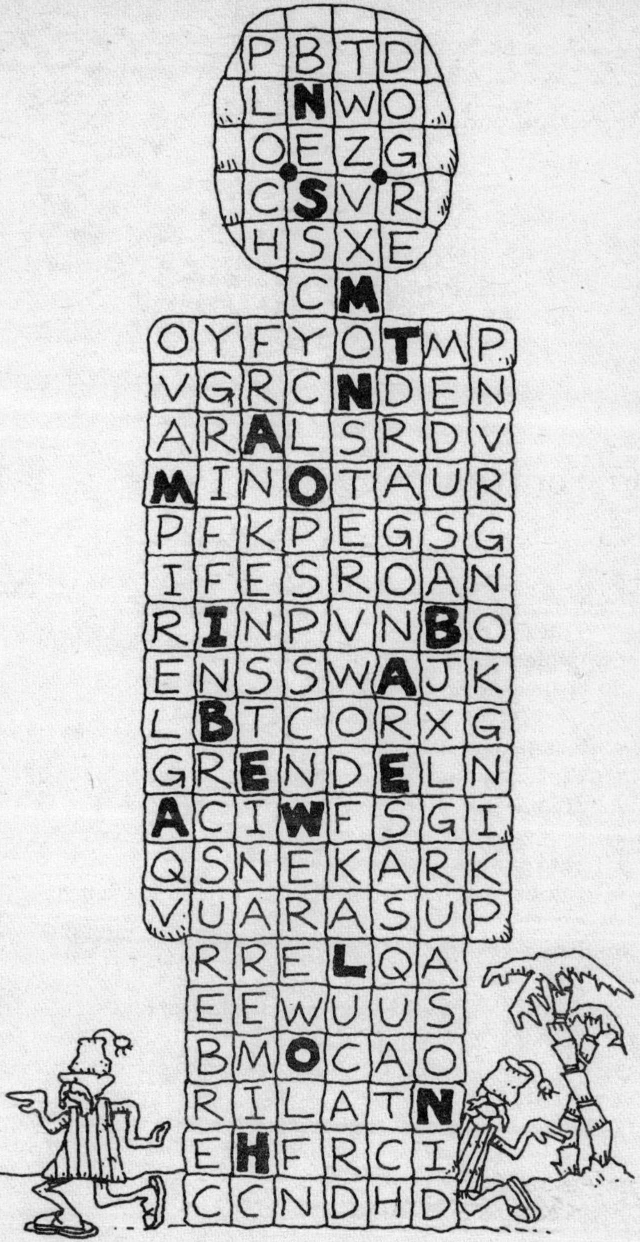
PBTD
LNWO
OEZG
CSVR
HSXE
CM
OYFYOTMP
VGRCNDEN
ARALSRDV
MINOTAUR
PFKPEGSG
IFESROAN
RINPVNBO
ENSSWAJK
LBTCORXG
GRENDELN
ACIWFSGI
QSNEKARK
VUARASUP
RRELQA
EEWUUS
BMOCAO
RILATN
EHFRCI
CCNDHD

## 61 For Wild Things

Test your knowledge of the countryside with this nature-lover's quiz.

**True or False?**
1. Centipedes have 100 legs.
2. Scarlet pimpernel flowers are always scarlet.
3. Dock leaves may ease nettle stings.
4. Snakes have no eyelids.
5. Great grey slugs mate in mid-air suspended on a thread of slime.
6. Seeds of yew trees are very poisonous.
7. Stink-horn is a hedgerow bush.
8. Cuckoo-pint was used by Elizabethans to starch their ruffs.
9. Earwigs can fly.
10. Only male mosquitos bite.
11. A farrier skins wild animals and sells their fur.
12. A badger's home is called a den.
13. Fly agaric is a fly that nests in cow dung.
14. A red admiral is a type of moth.
15. Touching the giant hogweed may produce a painful rash.

16 · White Dead-nettles give a sharp sting.
17 · Cuckoo-spit is froth spat out by cuckoos.
18 · A coypu is a small grey bat.
19 · A female fox is called a bitch.
20 · The red deer is Britain's largest land animal.

## 62 Mixed Doubles

Who are these well-known twosomes?

1 · A bolero made them champions.
2 · Twins who argued about a rattle.
3 · They were given white and brown bread and plum cake.
4 · Owners of a wonderful circus.
5 · Their shadows, spirits and ghosts have four wheels.
6 · Yellow submarine writers.
7 · Their shop sells St Michael.
8 · Creators of *Patience*, *HMS Pinafore* and *Pirates of Penzance*.
9 · They were suckled by a wolf and founded Rome.

10 · Presumably they met at Ujiji in Africa.
11 · They climbed high in 1953.
12 · Dr Nice and Mr Nasty were one and the same.
13 · They designed a royal wedding dress in 1981.
14 · They went to fill a pail and ended up pale and ill.
15 · A detective duo from Baker Street.
16 · The top Victorian couple.
17 · Twins who edited *The Guinness Book of Records*.
18 · They found a house made of sweets.
19 · They were a wham!
20 · Thomas the Tank Engine's carriages.

# 63 Signs of the Times

Do you know the international signs for these items? Match them up with the symbols below.

1. Parking.
2. Camping.
3. Inflammable.
4. This way up.
5. Picnic area.
6. Restaurant.
7. Keep dry.
8. Live Aid.
9. Lift.
10. Telephone.
11. Information.
12. Post Office.
13. Fragile. Handle with care.
14. World Wildlife Fund.
15. Disabled.
16. Airport.
17. Shower.
18. Keep away from heat.
19. Petrol.
20. First Aid.

# 64 A Winner Every Time

Have you ever won a prize? This quiz is about awards, trophies and prizes. If you get them right you can award yourself a pat on the head!

**Which sport do you associate with each of these prizes?**
1 · The Littlewoods Cup.
2 · The Calcutta Cup.
3 · The Ryder Cup.
4 · The America's Cup.
5 · The FIFA World Cup.
6 · The Wightman Cup.
7 · A Lonsdale Belt.
8 · The Whitbread Gold Cup.
9 · The Ashes.
10 · The Davis Cup.

11 · Are Variety Club Awards in the form of
   a) a gold cup
   b) a silver heart
   c) a statue of Shakespeare?

12 · Which member of the royal family gave his name to an award system for young people?
13 · How many records must be sold for a gold disc to be awarded?
14 · The American Academy Awards took their name from
   a) Oscar Hammerstein
   b) Oscar Wilde
   c) Somebody's uncle.

15 · In which TV programme is 'Dusty Bin' the prize that no one wants to win?
16 · Michelin stars are awarded to
   a) restaurants
   b) cinemas
   c) tyres.
17 · What form of transport might win 'The Blue Riband of the Atlantic'?
18 · Nobel left money for the introduction of some famous prizes. What was his first name? Was it
   a) Frederick

    b) Nigel
    c) Alfred?
19 · On which TV game show might you win a cheque book and pen?
20 · The Golden Rose of Montreux Festival awards prizes for excellence in which field? Is it
    a) the recording industry
    b) television
    c) gardening?

# 65 Let's Get Physical

Forget computers and robots – the human body is so amazing that it takes your breath away.

**True or False?**
1 · It takes ten months to grow a complete toe-nail.
2 · During the average life the heart beats about 2,000,000,000 times.

3 · The smallest muscle in the body is in the little toe.
4 · Skin is replaced by new tissue twice a year.
5 · Sixty-five per cent of our body weight is water.
6 · Every night you grow about 0.3 inches – and you shrink again in the morning.
7 · An adult has 100 bones and fewer than 50 joints.
8 · The human body is covered by about 5,000,000 hairs.
9 · Hair grows faster in winter.
10 · A snore has been known to match the sound of a pneumatic drill.
11 · When we cough, air rushes out at a speed of up to thirty m.p.h.
12 · In a lifetime, the average persons eats about fifty tonnes of food.
13 · Astronauts can grow about two inches when in flight.
14 · During exercise the pulse rate can drop from 200 to 70 beats per minute.
15 · The air sacs in our lungs would cover an area of 100 square metres if laid out flat.
16 · We lose about 100 hairs a day, but we also replace them.
17 · There are 2,500,000 pores in our skin.
18 · The tongue contains thirty taste buds.
19 · Twenty per cent of the oxygen we breathe is used by the brain.
20 · The average adult has three litres of blood in his or her body.

# 66 Score Bored?

Here are a score of questions based on the numbers one to twenty for you to score a score out of a score, or twenty out of twenty.

1 · By what title is the First Lord of the Treasury better known?
2 · Where the animals went in two by two.
3 · Three literary sisters wrote under the pseudonyms of Acton, Currer and Ellis Bell. Who are they better known as?
4 · Tongues can tell a total of four tastes. What are they?
5 · What are humorous five-line rhymes known as?
6 · In which English city were sextuplets born in 1983?
7 · What are the seven colours of the rainbow?
8 · The eighth largest island in the world, and one of the most densely populated, is in the North Atlantic Ocean. Which island is it?

9 · Which of the nine planets in our solar system is the largest?
10 · What athletic event has ten different sections?
11 · Whose official residence is 11 Downing Street?
12 · What starts on the 'Glorious 12th'?
13 · Which flag, also known as Old Glory, has thirteen stripes?
14 · In which sport can players use a maximum of fourteen pieces of equipment to hit the ball?
15 · And which game, developed at a public school in England, is played with fifteen on each side?
16 · The sixteenth president of the United States spoke of 'Government of the people, by the people, for the people'. Who was he?
17 · Which facial expression uses seventeen muscles – smiling or frowning?
18 · How much non-gold is there in eighteen-carat gold?
19 · Who was burned at the stake at the age of nineteen?
20 · Who fell asleep for twenty years on the Catskill Mountains?

# 67 Twenty Bright Ideas

In 1750 Jonas Hanway appeared on the streets of London carrying an umbrella. Everyone fell about laughing. Good ideas are not always appreciated straight away! See how much you know about these rather clever inventions.

### Which invention . . .
1 · by Tom Smith makes Christmas snappy?
2 · by Walter Hunt holds nappies in place?
3 · by Clarence Birdseye makes food last longer?
4 · by Isaac Singer has people in stitches?
5 · by King Camp Gillette produces a close shave?
6 · by Lord Belisha is rather flashy?
7 · by John Walker can light fires?
8 · by Alfred Nobel had an explosive effect?
9 · by Wilhelm Röntgen can see right through you?
10 · by Karl Nessler caused hair to curl?

**Which answer is correct?**

11 · Edison's first words on his recording machine were
   a) 'Mary had a little lamb'
   b) 'Little Bo-Peep'
   c) 'Who's a clever boy, then?'

12 · When Whitcomb Judson got fed up with lacing his boots,
   a) he bought slippers instead
   b) he tied them up with string
   c) he invented the zip.

13 · The first Christmas card showed
   a) a robin
   b) a family dinner
   c) a Christmas tree.

14 · Elisha Otis helped people to go up in the world by inventing
   a) a crane
   b) the helicopter
   c) the safety lift.

15 · Percy Shaw improved road safety by inventing
   a) cat's eyes
   b) pedestrian crossings
   c) spectacles.

**16** · Sir John Harington, the inventor of the WC, was
   a) an explorer
   b) a plumber
   c) a poet.
**17** · In 1620 James I inspected a new invention. It was
   a) a lifeboat
   b) a submarine
   c) a diving bell.
**18** · Radio telegraphy was used to capture
   a) Dr Crippen
   b) Jack the Ripper
   c) Al Capone.
**19** · The first city to have parking meters was
   a) Tokyo
   b) Birmingham
   c) Oklahoma.
**20** · The first living things to travel in a hot-air balloon were
   a) three rats
   b) a rooster, a sheep and a duck
   c) a cat, a dog and a cow.

# 68 On Safari

You are on safari in Africa. The dusty track winds off into the distance . . .

1. · You see a group of large cats hunting as a team. What are they?
2. · Over there is a baobab tree with the bark stripped off. Who did it? Was it
   a) an elephant
   b) a giraffe
   c) a zebra?

3. · Your guide points out a secretary bird. It got its name because
   a) it sounds like a typewriter
   b) its head feathers look like quill pens
   c) it makes its nest from paper.
4. · Wow! There goes the fastest land animal in the world. What was it?

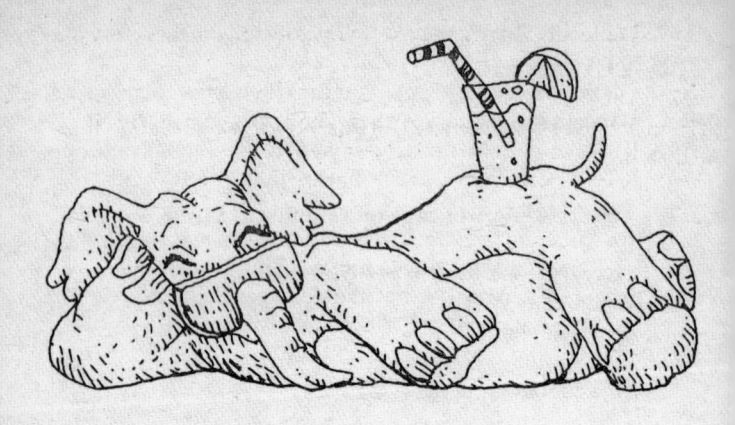

5 · And there's a giraffe. Which has the largest number of neck bones – a giraffe, a man or a mouse?
6 · You see a leopard – or is it a panther. What's the difference?
7 · Lying in the grass are some ostriches, the world's largest birds. Is it true that they fight with their toes?
8 · What on earth is that six-metre-tall pillar?
9 · Beware the black rhino – its horns look nasty! What are they made of? . . .
10 · . . . and what would happen if they fell off?
11 · Why have some animals in that buffalo herd got curved horns and some got straight ones?
12 · In the sky are some vultures. What do jackals, vultures and hyenas have in common?
13 · You are near a lake. Why is that hippo spinning its tail round and round?
14 · And why are those crocodiles lying on the bank with their mouths open? Are they
   a) waiting for their dinner to walk in
   b) keeping cool
   c) allowing birds to clean their teeth for them?
15 · Is it true that a mother crocodile carries her babies in her mouth?

16 · Look out! There's a snake! Why is its tongue flickering in and out?
17 · On that branch is a lizard that can change the colour of its skin and swivel each eye independently. What is it?
18 · If you go deep into the forest you may see a family group led by a large silverback. What are they?
19 · And what is that? Its cheeks are blue, its nose and rump are red and it has a yellow beard!
20 · The last animal you see before reaching camp is very strange too. It has a snout like a pig, ears like a donkey, a tail like a kangaroo and clawed feet. What is it?

## 69 Round the World

How good is your geography? Go globe-trotting and find the odd one out in each group.

1 · Nebraska, Panama, Texas, Ohio.
2 · Etna, Vesuvius, Krakatoa, Old Faithful.

3 · Paris, Madrid, New York, Rome.
4 · Amazon, Panama, Suez, Grand.
5 · Mediterranean, Pacific, Atlantic, Indian.
6 · Monsoon, Mistral, Gulf Stream, Chinook.
7 · Amazon, Orinoco, Nile, Paraná.
8 · Hudson, Cod, Biscay, Bengal.
9 · Arctic, Iceland, Greenland, Antarctic.
10 · Shanghai, Peking, Nanking, Osaka.
11 · Pampas, Sahara, Negev, Kalahari.
12 · Yugoslavia, Switzerland, Austria, Hungary.
13 · Niagara, Superior, Angel, Victoria.
14 · Grand Canyon, Cheddar Gorge, Rocky Mountains, Khyber Pass.
15 · CD, NL, DK, E.
16 · Europe, India, Africa, Asia.
17 · Hawaiian Islands, Fiji Islands, Cook Islands, Canary Islands.
18 · Titicaca, Lucerne, St Lawrence, Huron.
19 · Cotopaxi, Eiger, Everest, Kilimanjaro.
20 · Darwin, Sydney, Perth, Wellington.

## 70 In Their Own Words

**Who said . . .**
1. 'Odds fish I am an ugly fellow!'
   a) Charles II
   b) Bonnie Prince Charlie
   c) Prince Charles.
2. 'We are not amused.'
   a) Victoria Wood
   b) Victoria Principal
   c) Queen Victoria.
3. 'That's one small step for a man, one giant leap for mankind.'
   a) Neil Kinnock
   b) Neil Armstrong
   c) Neil Diamond.
4. 'History is more or less bunk.'
   a) Harrison Ford
   b) Anna Ford
   c) Henry Ford.

5 · 'Dr Livingstone, I presume?'
   a) Stanley Matthews
   b) Sir Henry Stanley
   c) Stanley Baxter.

**Fighting talk! Match the speech to the speaker. Who said . . .**
6 · 'Never in the field of human conflict was so much owed by so many to so few.'
7 · 'An army marches on its stomach.'
8 · 'England expects that every man will do his duty.'
9 · 'There's plenty of time to win this game and to thrash the Spaniards too.'
10 · 'Up Guards and at them again!'

Francis Drake . . . Winston Churchill . . . Napoleon . . . Lord Nelson . . . Duke of Wellington

**Who exclaimed . . .**
11 · 'Sing Ho! for the life of a bear!'
12 · 'Curiouser and curiouser!'
13 · 'O bliss! O poop-poop! O my! O my!'
14 · 'Pieces of eight! Pieces of eight!'
15 · 'Oliver Twist has asked for more!'

**And finally, whose were these famous last words?**
16 · 'I shall hear in heaven.'
17 · 'The executioner is, I believe, very expert, and my neck is very slender.'
18 · 'Et tu, Brute?'
19 · 'I am just going outside and may be some time.'
20 · 'Die, my dear doctor! That's the last thing I shall do.'

Julius Caesar . . . Lawrence Oates . . . Beethoven . . . Anne Boleyn . . . Lord Palmerston

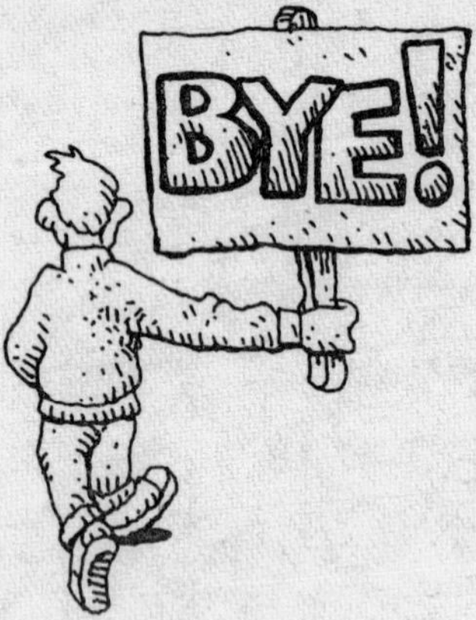
BYE!

# Answers

## 2 Hidden Treasure

1 · Gold.  2 · Open Sesame.  3 · *Treasure Island*.
4 · Opals.  5 · Ruby.  6 · Amber.  7 · Tutankhamun.
8 · Tower of London.  9 · Lucky dip.  10 · Emerald.
11 · Silver.  12 · Necklace.  13 · Aladdin.  14 · Knox.
15 · Eggs.  16 · Rings.  17 · Ivory.  18 · Diamonds.
19 · Gems.  20 · El Dorado.
GO TO RATTLESNAKE RIDGE

## 3 Busman's Holiday?

1 · The *Tardis*.  2 · A whale.  3 · A transformed pumpkin.  4 · Black Bess.  5 · A pea-green boat.  6 · The *Millennium Falcon*.  7 · *Apollo 11*.  8 · A bicycle made for two.  9 · A giant peach.  10 · *Virgin Atlantic*.
11 · *Kon-Tiki*.  12 · *Swallow*.  13 · The *Mayflower*.
14 · Aslan the lion.  15 · *Chitty-Chitty-Bang-Bang*.
16 · *Nautilus*.  17 · A sieve.  18 · *Bluebird*.
19 · HMS *Bounty*.  20 · A tub.

## 4 Women of the World

1 · They were all film stars when children.  2 · They are well-known dress designers.  3 · They have opera singing in common.  4 · They have all been heads of government.
5 · They are known for their writing on cookery.  6 · They have all illustrated children's books.  7 · They were all queens.
8 · They are all famous in the world of aviation.  9 · They have all

written children's books.    10 · They are all dolls.    11 · They are all female pop groups.    12 · They have riding in common.    13 · They are all athletes.    14 · They were all film stars.    15 · They have all been presenters on *Blue Peter*.    16 · They are well known as jazz singers.    17 · They are all comediennes.    18 · They are all actresses.    19 · They have dancing in common.    20 · They all present and report the news.

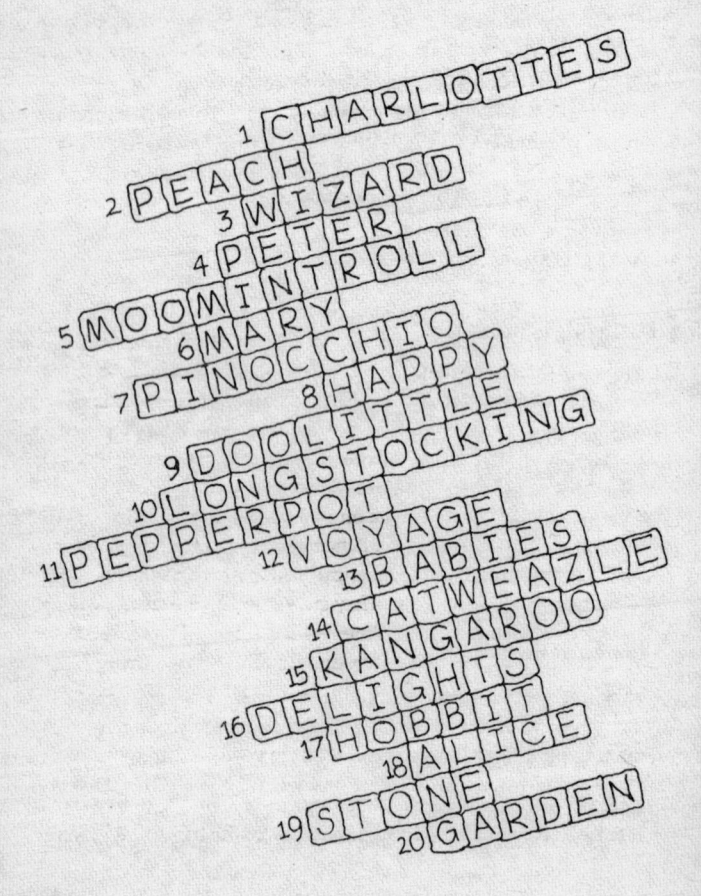

1 CHARLOTTES
2 PEACH
3 WIZARD
4 PETER
5 MOOMINTROLL
6 MARY
7 PINOCCHIO
8 HAPPY
9 DOOLITTLE
10 LONGSTOCKING
11 PEPPERPOT
12 VOYAGE
13 BABIES
14 CATWEAZLE
15 KANGAROO
16 DELIGHTS
17 HOBBIT
18 ALICE
19 STONE
20 GARDEN

## 6 Feathered Friends

**1** · The white-headed American eagle.   **2** · The dove.   **3** · The peacock.   **4** · The raven. It is said that if they fly away the Tower will fall, so their wings are clipped to prevent this disaster.
**5** · The phoenix.   **6** · Chicken-Licken.   **7** · Polynesia, the parrot in *Doctor Dolittle* by Hugh Lofting.   **8** · Owl in *The House at Pooh Corner* by A. A. Milne.   **9** · Hickety-Pickety.   **10** · Peter and Paul.   **11** · The ostrich.   **12** · Cuckoos.
**13** · Humming-birds.   **14** · Storing food.   **15** · The peregrine falcon. It can fly at over 350 k.p.h.!   **16** · True. Many birds swallow grit which grinds the food up inside their gizzards.   **17** · True. Most birds moult at least once a year.   **18** · True. Only a penguin can survive an Antarctic winter with temperatures of 40° below freezing.   **19** · True. The air is stored at the wide end of the egg.   **20** · False. Some can't, including the ostrich, rhea and emu.


## 7 Piggy Bank Posers

**1** · False. It is the Duke of Wellington.   **2** · True. It began in 1950.   **3** · False. It has seven.   **4** · True. The *banco* or bench was used by money-lenders.   **5** · True. It was issued by the Bank of Stockholm in Sweden.   **6** · False. In the legend everything turned to gold.   **7** · True.   **8** · True.   **9** · True. They are worth about 1¢ each.   **10** · True. It began as a temporary measure in 1799.   **11** · False. It produces 8,000,000,000 coins per year.
**12** · True. Decimalization began on 15 February 1971.   **13** · False. They were originally American kitchen jars made from Pygg clay.
**14** · True. It was used in the American sense to mean someone with $1,000,000,000.   **15** · False. They are signed by the chief cashier of the Bank of England.   **16** · True.   **17** · True. They called it 'flying money'.   **18** · False. It is the escudo.   **19** · True.
**20** · True.


## 8 The Wild West

**1** · a).   **2** · c).   **3** · a).   **4** · c).   **5** · b).   **6** · a).
**7** · False. It contained food and provisions for the trip.   **8** · False.

They were used for marking cattle.   **9** · True. He was later shot down by Sheriff Pat Garrett.   **10** · False. It is land given to the Indians for their own use.   **11** · True. That is how he got the nickname.   **12** · False. They built up a stagecoach network.   **13** · True. It was purchased in 1803 and more than doubled the size of the US.   **14** · True. He was defeated by Sitting Bull's forces on 25 June 1876.   **15** · False. It only took a day!   **16** · True. The Pony Express advertisement called for 'Young skinny wiry fellows, not over eighteen . . . willing to risk death daily.'   **17** · False. 1849 was the year of the Gold Rush and the men who joined it were called the Forty-niners.   **18** · True. Wyatt and his brothers shot and killed two of the Clanton gang and the others fled.   **19** · False. A totem pole is a large tree trunk decorated with painted carvings as a memorial to ancestors.   **20** · True. She was a sharp-shooter and toured with Buffalo Bill's Wild West Show.

## 10  Driving Range

**1** · Swimming.   **2** · Rowing.   **3** · Boxing.   **4** · Snooker.   **5** · Netball.   **6** · Badminton.   **7** · Archery.   **8** · Tennis.   **9** · Wrestling.   **10** · Trampolining.   **11** · Cricket.   **12** · Diving.   **13** · Bowls.   **14** · Billiards.   **15** · Football.   **16** · Polo.   **17** · Hockey.   **18** · Lacrosse.   **19** · Skiing.   **20** · Squash. The Spanish golfer is SEVERIANO BALLESTEROS.

## 11  The Best of Enemies

**1** · Walter, the softy.   **2** · Sheriff of Nottingham.   **3** · Skeletor.   **4** · Dr No.   **5** · Flashman.   **6** · Det. Sgt. Chisholm.   **7** · Erich von Stalhein.   **8** · Wicked Witch of the West.   **9** · Bluto.   **10** · Cut-Throat Jake.   **11** · Captain Hook.   **12** · Darth Vader.   **13** · Shere Khan.   **14** · Mr Boff.   **15** · Tom.   **16** · Sylvester.   **17** · Cliff Barnes.   **18** · Dr Doom.   **19** · Lex Luthor.   **20** · Catwoman.

## 12 Ready for Take-off

1 · Pan Am to Washington.   2 · El Al to Jerusalem.   3 · Air France to Paris.   4 · Qantas to Canberra.   5 · Swissair to Berne.   6 · KLM to Amsterdam.   7 · Lufthansa to Bonn.   8 · Aer Lingus to Dublin.   9 · Icelandair to Reykjavik.   10 · Egyptair to Cairo.   11 · Air Canada to Ottawa.   12 · British Airways to London.   13 · Finnair to Helsinki.   14 · Sabena to Brussels.   15 · Iberia to Madrid.   16 · Olympic Airways to Athens.   17 · Air India to Delhi.   18 · Alitalia to Rome.   19 · Japan Airlines to Tokyo.   20 · Aeroflot to Moscow.

Concorde is flying SUPERSONIC TO HEATHROW.

## 13 Men of the World

1 · They all work with puppets – Sooty, Orville and Emu.   2 · They have all been British prime ministers.   3 · They are well known as magicians.   4 · They all play the violin.   5 · They have all played the part of Dr Who.   6 · Each one was assassinated.   7 · They are all snooker players.   8 · The three Wise Men traditionally have these names.   9 · They are all famous as world champion racing drivers.   10 · They are all ballet dancers.   11 · They are all tennis players.   12 · Each one's invention has been named after him.   13 · They are all golfers.   14 · They have all hosted chat shows on television.   15 · They have film directing in common.   16 · They are all famous as outlaws.   17 · All of them are artists.   18 · They all play cricket.   19 · They have all written successful musicals.   20 · They are all footballers.

## 14 Twenty Answers for High Fliers

1 · Peter Pan.   2 · Icarus, whose wings of wax melted.   3 · Wilbur Wright.   4 · A swallow.   5 · Mary Poppins.   6 · The Snowman.   7 · Charles Lindbergh in the first solo non-stop flight across the Atlantic.   8 · Meg in the books by Jan Pienkowski.   9 · Captain Kirk and his crew in the TV series *Star*

*Trek*.   10 · Superman.   11 · France and Britain.   12 · The hot-air balloon in the story by Jules Verne.   13 · It was a British airship.   14 · A helium-filled balloon that crossed the USA in 1981.   15 · Biggles in the books by Captain W. E. Johns.   16 · The Red Baron.   17 · Dumbo.   18 · The sycamore tree produces seeds that twirl like helicopter blades.   19 · A vertical, short take-off and landing plane.   20 · By the most direct route.

## 15 Royal Progress

1 · Arthur.   2 · Camelot.   3 · Canute.   4 · Harold. 5 · William.   6 · Richard (I).   7 · Windsor.   8 · John. 9 · Hampton Court.   10 · Henry (VIII).   11 · Elizabeth (I). 12 · Charles (I).   13 · Whitehall.   14 · Victoria. 15 · Buckingham.   16 · Margaret.   17 · Andrew. 18 · Diana.   19 · Harry.   20 · York.
The Queen is GIVING OUT MAUNDY MONEY. Maundy money is given by the sovereign to the number of elderly men and women that corresponds to the sovereign's age. In 1987 Queen Elizabeth II was sixty-one, so the gift was given to sixty-one men and sixty-one women. The money is specially minted for the occasion.

## 16 Match the Music

1 · Olivia Newton John.   2 · David Bowie.   3 · Grace Jones. 4 · Prince.   5 · Tina Turner.   6 · Elvis Presley.   7 · Cliff Richard.   8 · Paul McCartney.   9 · Madonna.   10 · Roger Daltry.   11 · *The Sound of Music*.   12 · *Jungle Book*. 13 · *Evita*.   14 · *Mary Poppins*.   15 · *Watership Down*. 16 · *Snow White and the Seven Dwarfs*.   17 · *South Pacific*. 18 · *Cats*.   19 · *Oliver!*   20 · *Romancing the Stone*.

## 17 Tree Word-search

MIGHTY OAKS FROM LITTLE ACORNS GROW.

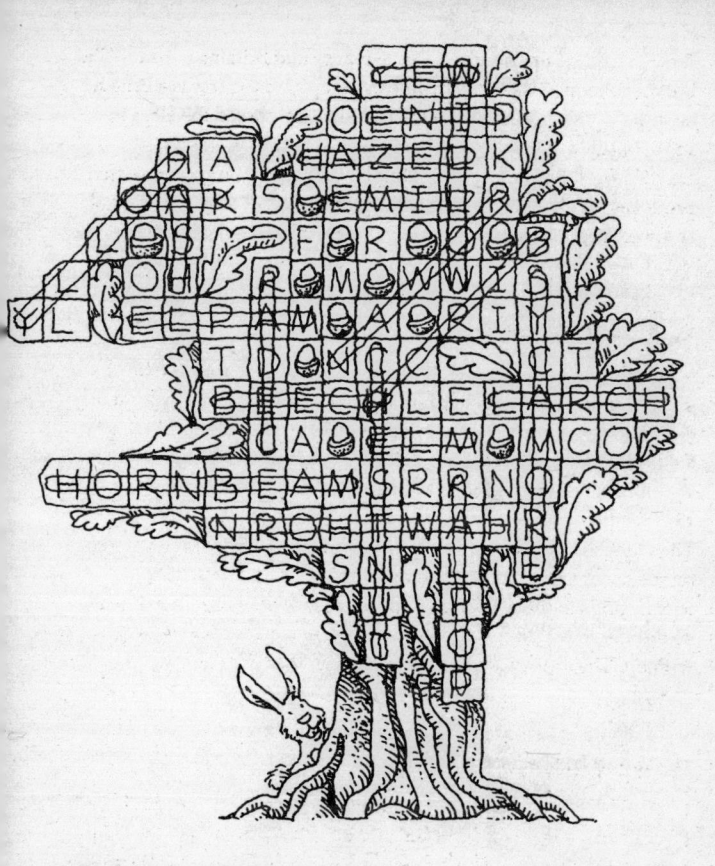

## 18 Back to the Nursery

1 · Boy Blue.  2 · Solomon Grundy.  3 · Lucy Locket.
4 · Dr Foster.  5 · Simple Simon.  6 · Polly Flinders.
7 · King Cole.  8 · The Duke of York.  9 · Peter Piper.
10 · Yankee Doodle.  11 · Mother Hubbard.
12 · Tommy Tittlemouse.  13 · The Knave of Hearts.
14 · Bobbie Shaftoe.  15 · Humpty Dumpty.
16 · Queen Caroline.  17 · Tommy Tucker.
18 · Betty Blue.  19 · Georgie Porgie.  20 · Jack Sprat.

133

## 19 As Seen on TV

1 · *The A Team.*  2 · *Dallas.*  3 · *Only Fools and Horses.*
4 · *Crossroads.*  5 · *Coronation Street.*  6 · *Happy Days.*
7 · *Postman Pat.*  8 · *Last of the Summer Wine.*
9 · *Star Trek.*  10 · *Fawlty Towers.*  11 · *The Young Ones.*
12 · *Rainbow.*  13 · *Dynasty.*  14 · *Worzel Gummidge.*
15 · *Emmerdale Farm.*  16 · *Hi-de-Hi!*  17 · *EastEnders.*
18 · *Brush Strokes.*  19 · *'Allo 'Allo.*  20 · *Grange Hill.*

## 20 Criss-cross Words

1 · Apple.  2 · Arrow.  3 · Enrol.  4 · Limit.
5 · Woman.  6 · Nests.  7 · Tests.  8 · Story.
9 · Shore.  10 · Empty.  11 · Exist.  12 · Error.
13 · Throw.  14 · Wrath.  15 · Roast.  16 · Tramp.
17 · Heals.  18 · Sprat.  19 · Party.  20 · Yacht.

## 21 Crack the Word

1 · Bottle.  2 · Door.  3 · Skin.  4 · Bath.
5 · Wave.  6 · Fire.  7 · Cross.  8 · Light.
9 · Table.  10 · Dog.  11 · Baby.  12 · Box.
13 · Chocolate.  14 · Top.  15 · Friend.  16 · Clock.
17 · Stick.  18 · Fly.  19 · Trap.  20 · Paper.

## 22 Arty-crafty

1 · Mona Lisa.  2 · The Umbrellas.  3 · Sunflowers.
4 · Guernica.  5 · The Night Watch.  6 · An illusion in painting.  7 · Wall painting on wet plaster.  8 · Pictures made from small tiles.  9 · Pictures in stitches.  10 · Pictures inlaid in wood.  11 · Sculptor.  12 · Architect.  13 · Wood carver.  14 · Potter.  15 · Garden designer.  16 · Scribe. It is a type of paper.  17 · Artist. It is a type of paint.  18 · Potter. It is used to decorate pots.  19 · Sculptor.  20 · Printer.

## 23 Twenty Running Answers

1 · Wee Willie Winkie.   2 · Cinderella.   3 · The mouse in Hickory, Dickory, Dock.   4 · Three blind mice.   5 · A tortoise.   6 · Tom, the Piper's son.   7 · Alice from *Alice's Adventures in Wonderland* by Lewis Carroll.   8 · Tom in *The Water-Babies* by Charles Kingsley.   9 · Mercury.   10 · Oliver Twist in the book by Charles Dickens.   11 · A runner bean.   12 · A member of the first regular police force in London.   13 · A zebra.   14 · A marathon.   15 · The competitor is disqualified.   16 · Sebastian Coe.   17 · A baton.   18 · Roger Bannister ran the mile in 3 minutes and 59.4 seconds in 1954.   19 · The Derby.   20 · To run one kilometre in five minutes.

## 24 Twenty Jumping Answers

1 · The cow.   2 · Sitting Bull.   3 · The kangaroo.   4 · Hop, skip and jump.   5 · The first footstep on the moon.   6 · Look!   7 · Evel Knievel.   8 · Glass fibre.   9 · The Grand National.   10 · Figure skating.   11 · Diagonally.   12 · All the horses that jumped clear in the first round of a showjumping competition jump a second round against the clock.   13 · Three-day event jumping.   14 · Trampolining.   15 · A candlestick.   16 · Ten.   17 · To connect the live battery from one car to the flat battery of another in order to get it to start.   18 · High jumping.   19 · The Dutch.   20 · It is laid out according to the number of lines – either horizontal, vertical or diagonal – in each fence. The order is thus f), a), c), d), b), e) or vice versa.

## 25 Twenty Standing Still Answers

1 · Nelson.   2 · A soldier.   3 · Popeye.   4 · Queen Victoria. Her statue stands outside Buckingham Palace.   5 · The best man.   6 · General Custer.   7 · Father William in the poem by Lewis Carroll.   8 · A highwayman.   9 · France, in 1886.   10 · To keep a sentry dry in bad weather.

11 · Weightlifting.   12 · Hyde Park.   13 · The Monument.   14 · The statue of Peter Pan.   15 · The Little Mermaid, who is based on the Hans Andersen character.   16 · A sculpture of the heads of four American presidents.   17 · Sydney Opera House.   18 · Empire State Building, New York.   19 · St Paul's Cathedral, London.   20 · Eiffel Tower, Paris.

## 27 Heroes and Heroines

1 · Flora Macdonald.   2 · Amy Johnson.   3 · Joan of Arc.
4 · Gladys Aylward.   5 · Grace Darling, the lighthouse keeper's daughter.   6 · Elizabeth Fry.   7 · Florence Nightingale.
8 · Boadicea.   9 · Anne Frank. She later died in the concentration camp at Belsen.   10 · Emmeline Pankhurst.   11 · Alexander the Great.   12 · Davy Crockett, 'King of the Wild Frontier'.
13 · William Tell.   14 · Charles Lindbergh.   15 · David Livingstone.   16 · Horatio Nelson.   17 · Martin Luther King.   18 · Albert Schweitzer.   19 · Thomas E. Lawrence, 'Lawrence of Arabia'.   20 · Roald Amundsen. He beat Scott to it.

## 28 Twenty Fruit Facts

1 · False. Raisins are dried grapes.   2 · True. The Spanish discoverers of the West Indian tree gave it this name.   3 · True. The tree reached Portugal in the 1630s.   4 · False. Cider is made from apples.   5 · True.   6 · True.   7 · Nell Gwyn sold oranges to theatre-goers in the seventeenth century.   8 · True.
9 · True. A tomato is the fruit of the tomato plant and contains its seeds.   10 · True.   11 · False. Perrier is the name of a brand of natural mineral water.   12 · False. They grow on bushes.
13 · True.   14 · False. The tree does not exist.   15 · True.
16 · False. On the contrary, it is the most common wild fruit.
17 · True. A lot of bananas grow there!   18 · True, though white wine may be made from white or red grapes with the skins removed.   19 · True.   20 · False. It is made from cherries.

## 29 Characters in Search of a Bargain

1 · Hat costing 10/6.   2 · The sword Excalibur.   3 · Seven little hats.   4 · Bottle of frobscottle.   5 · Litter bin.   6 · Washing powder.   7 · Book of inventions.   8 · Pipe.   9 · Dog food.   10 · Catapult.   11 · House insurance.   12 · Magic beans.   13 · Mayor's hat.   14 · Duffel coat.   15 · Key.   16 · New top hat.   17 · Honey.   18 · Elastoplast.   19 · Train set.   20 · Pot of slime.

## 30 Celebrations!

1 · Harvest.   2 · Pancakes.   3 · Yom Kippur.   4 · July.   5 · Easter.   6 · Patrick.   7 · *Mardi gras*.   8 · George.   9 · Bonfires.   10 · New Year.   11 · May Day.   12 · Andrew.   13 · Passover.   14 · Christmas Eve.   15 · Diwali.   16 · Hallowe'en.   17 · First Footer.   18 · Boxing Day.   19 · Hogmanay.   20 · Valentine.
The bed is an APPLE-PIE BED – it's an APRIL FOOL!

## 31 Beastly Books

1 · Brer Rabbit in *The Wonderful Tar-Baby* by Joel Chandler Harris.   2 · Eeyore in *Winnie-the-Pooh* by A. A. Milne.   3 · The Elephant's Child in *Just So Stories* by Rudyard Kipling.   4 · The crocodile in *Peter Pan* by J. M. Barrie.   5 · The Cowardly Lion in *The Wonderful Wizard of Oz* by L. Frank Baum.   6 · Hazel, Fiver, Bigwig and a company of rabbits in *Watership Down* by Richard Adams.   7 · Pongo in *The One Hundred and One Dalmatians* by Dodie Smith.   8 · Paddington Bear in *A Bear Called Paddington* by Michael Bond.   9 · Luath, Tao and Bodger in *The Incredible Journey* by Sheila Burnford.   10 · Skimbleshanks the Railway Cat in *Old Possum's Book of Practical Cats* by T. S. Eliot.   11 · Bambi in the book by Felix Salten.   12 · Charlotte in *Charlotte's Web* by E. B. White.   13 · Rat in *Wind in the Willows* by Kenneth Grahame.   14 · Aslan in *The Lion, the Witch and the Wardrobe* by C. S. Lewis.   15 · Fantastic Mr Fox in the book by Roald Dahl.   16 · Mog in *Meg and Mog* by Helen Nicoll.   17 · Jess in the stories by John

Cunliffe.   **18** · Razzle in the stories by Joan Eadington.
**19** · Cap'n Flint, the parrot, in *Treasure Island* by Robert Louis
Stevenson.   **20** · Teddy Robinson in the books by Joan G.
Robinson.

## 32 Quick Change

**1** · Six lizards in Cinderella.   **2** · An ogre.   **3** · Max in *Where the Wild Things Are* by Maurice Sendak.   **4** · Clark Kent becomes Superman.   **5** · Mildred Hubble in the story by Jill Murphy.
**6** · The Ugly Duckling.   **7** · SuperTed.   **8** · The Duchess's baby.   **9** · Pinocchio in the story by Carlo Collodi.
**10** · Bananaman.   **11** · Elaine Page.   **12** · David Bowie.
**13** · Paul Jones, who hosts television's *Beat the Teacher*.
**14** · Freddie Mercury, the singer with Queen.   **15** · Boy George of Culture Club.   **16** · Elton John.   **17** · Ringo Starr of the Beatles.   **18** · Cliff Richard.   **19** · Sting.   **20** · Madonna.

## 33 Happy Families

**1** · Queen Elizabeth II.   **2** · Wilma Flintstone.   **3** · Princess Leia.   **4** · John McEnroe.   **5** · Andrew Lloyd Webber.
**6** · Donald Duck.   **7** · Paula Yates.   **8** · Chris Evert.
**9** · Paddington Bear.   **10** · Brian Clough.   **11** · Margaret Thatcher.   **12** · King Arthur.   **13** · Henry VIII.   **14** · Kirk Douglas.   **15** · James in *James and the Giant Peach*.
**16** · Mould.   **17** · Harpo Marx.   **18** · Mary I.   **19** · Maggie Philbin.   **20** · Princess Margaret.

## 35 Think Small

**1** · Little Jack Horner.   **2** · Little Lord Fauntleroy in the book by Frances Hodgson Burnett.   **3** · Little Miss Muffet.   **4** · General Tom Thumb.   **5** · Sleepy, Happy, Doc, Dopey, Bashful, Sneezy and Grumpy.   **6** · The Borrowers in the books by Mary Norton.   **7** · Little Red Riding Hood.   **8** · Meg, Jo, Beth and Amy in *Little Women* by Louisa M. Alcott.   **9** · Tiny Tim in *A Christmas Carol* by Charles Dickens.   **10** · Alice in *Alice's Adventures* *in Wonderland* by Lewis Carroll.   **11** · The small inhabitants of Lilliput, whom Gulliver met in *Gulliver's Travels* by Jonathan Swift.   **12** · *The Little Engine that Could* by Watty Piper.   **13** · Little John.   **14** · Little Jenny Wren in *Sing a Song of Sixpence*.   **15** · Small people, whom Dorothy met in the land of Oz in *The Wonderful Wizard of Oz* by L. Frank Baum.   **16** · Little Bo-Peep.   **17** · Little Orphan Annie.   **18** · The Little Match Girl in the story by Hans Andersen.   **19** · The Three Little Pigs.   **20** · Little Grey Rabbit in the books by Alison Uttley.

## 36 Larger than Life

**1** · Bigwig.   **2** · Big Ears.   **3** · Big Ben.   **4** · The big ship.   **5** · A big wheel.   **6** · The giant in *Jack and the Beanstalk*.   **7** · Pinocchio in the story by Carlo Collodi.   **8** · Goliath.   **9** · The enormous turnip.   **10** · The BFG in the story by Roald Dahl.   **11** · The Tinder Box by Hans Andersen.   **12** · Jaws.   **13** · Gulliver in the story by Jonathan Swift.   **14** · The selfish giant in the story by Oscar Wilde.   **15** · George's marvellous medicine in the story by Roald Dahl.   **16** · a).   **17** · c).   **18** · b).   **19** · c).   **20** · b).

## 37 Criss-cross Words

**1** · Start.   **2** · Spoil.   **3** · Troop.   **4** · Plant.   **5** · Least.   **6** · Truce.   **7** · Truth.   **8** · Hotel.   **9** · Extol.   **10** · Level.   **11** · Toast.   **12** · Train.   **13** · Trail.   **14** · Lager.   **15** · Night.   **16** · Think.   **17** · Raise.   **18** · Enemy.   **19** · Kneel.   **20** · Lanky.

## 38 Pet Shop Posers

**1** · Guinea pig.   **2** · Rabbit.   **3** · Pony.   **4** · Goldfish.   **5** · Duck.   **6** · True. Their eyes are shut for the first few days.   **7** · False. Although they belong to the same family as the rabbit, they are a different animal.   **8** · False. The turkey is one of the least intelligent of birds.   **9** · False. Their eyes are blue.   **10** · True. Although she owns corgis, the Queen is not required to hold a licence

for them.   **11** · Millet seed.   **12** · Oats.
**13** · Greenflies.   **14** · Sunflower seeds.   **15** · A bone.
**16** · The snake lives in the vivarium.   **17** · The bees live in the hive.   **18** · The fish lives in the aquarium.   **19** · The doves live in the dovecote.   **20** · The rabbit lives in the hutch.

## 39  The Show Must Go On!

**1** · Stage.   **2** · Shakespeare.   **3** · Greece.   **4** · Opera.
**5** · Full house.   **6** · Stalls.   **7** · Wings.   **8** · Cast.
**9** · Prompt.   **10** · Programme.   **11** · Broadway.
**12** · Flies.   **13** · Interval.   **14** · Footlights.   **15** · Ballet.
**16** · Globe.   **17** · Pantomime.   **18** · Box office.
**19** · Circle.   **20** · Actor.
On stage tonight is THE PHANTOM OF THE OPERA.

## 40  All Dressed Up

**1** · He is a morris dancer from England.   **2** · She is from the Netherlands.   **3** · He is from Greece and is a guard.   **4** · He is from Mexico.   **5** · She is a dancer from Thailand.   **6** · The hat belongs to 5.   **7** · The hat belongs to 3.   **8** · The hat belongs to 2.   **9** · The hat belongs to 4.   **10** · The hat belongs to 1.
**11** · Max in *Where the Wild Things Are* by Maurice Sendak.
**12** · The Emperor in *The Emperor's New Clothes* by Hans Andersen.   **13** · Rupert Bear, the creation of Mary Tourtel.
**14** · Cruella de Vil in *The One Hundred and One Dalmatians* by Dodie Smith.   **15** · Peter Rabbit in the book by Beatrix Potter.
**16** · John in 'Happiness' in *When We Were Very Young* by A. A. Milne.   **17** · Joseph.   **18** · Noddy, created by Enid Blyton.
**19** · The Quangle-Wangle in the poem by Edward Lear.
**20** · Dorothy in *The Wonderful Wizard of Oz* by L. Frank Baum.

## 41  Come to the Concert

**1** · Cornet.   **2** · Bach.   **3** · Flute.   **4** · Harp.
**5** · Recorder.   **6** · Cello.   **7** · Drum.   **8** · Triangle.
**9** · Beethoven.   **10** · Tuba.   **11** · Harpsichord.

12 · Xylophone.   13 · Music.   14 · Piccolo.
15 · Violin.   16 · Philharmonic.   17 · Tambourine.
18 · Conductor.   19 · Mozart.   20 · Cymbals.
The annual event is THE PROMENADE CONCERTS.

## 42  Twenty Superlative Answers

1 · John McEnroe.   2 · Julie Andrews in the film *Mary Poppins*.   3 · Billy Connolly.   4 · Batman.
5 · Aladdin.   6 · Charles Dickens.   7 · George in the story by Roald Dahl.   8 · Concorde.   9 · American football.   10 · A very bright star.   11 · Mohammed Ali.   12 · The Stars and Stripes, the US flag.   13 · The Rocky Mountains.
14 · China.   15 · Coral.   16 · It was the Barnum and Bailey Circus.   17 · Christopher Reeve.   18 · They form part of the boundary between the USA and Canada.   19 · It was held in Hyde Park in 1851.   20 · In the night sky. It is a constellation.

## 43  Through the Centuries

1 · Boadicea.   2 · Hadrian.   3 · Chinese.
4 · Constantine.   5 · Patrick.   6 · Mohammed.
7 · Canterbury.   8 · Vikings.   9 · Alfred.
10 · Ethelred.   11 · Domesday.   12 · Samurai.
13 · Kubla.   14 · The Black Death.   15 · India.
16 · Michelangelo.   17 · Taj Mahal.   18 · James Cook.
19 · Gold.   20 · Titanic.

## 44  Tourist Attractions

1 · Stonehenge.   2 · Cheddar.   3 · Ness.   4 · Taj Mahal.   5 · Scone.   6 · Brasilia.   7 · Colosseum.
8 · Sphinx.   9 · Pompeii.   10 · Olympia.
11 · Disneyland.   12 · Osborne House.
13 · Notre-Dame.   14 · Offa's Dike.   15 · Wailing Wall.
16 · Atlantis.   17 · China.   18 · Peter.   19 · Knossos.
20 · Istanbul.
The twenty-first sight is THE ACROPOLIS OF ATHENS.

## 46 Something Fishy

1 · True.   2 · False. They occur at the time of the full moon.
3 · True. They fix themselves head downwards on to a hard surface.   4 · True. They may have a holdfast attaching them to a rock.   5 · True. Exactly the same place!   6 · False. They feed by filtering sea-water through their pores.   7 · True. They regrow over a period of time.   8 · True. They start female and become male later.   9 · True.   10 · True.   11 · False. They are bluish black and become red when cooked.   12 · True.
13 · True.   14 · True.   15 · True. They easily grow replacements.   16 · False. It is a type of fish.   17 · True. They are very quick too!   18 · True. Holiday-makers sometimes trample on their nests by mistake.   19 · False. Unlike land slugs, sea slugs are attractive animals.   20 · True. It does it to confuse the enemy.


## 47 Oddities

1 · Amplifier. The others are used in photography.   2 · Glass. The others are gems.   3 · Basmati is a form of rice and the others are types of sugar.   4 · Gallon. The others are metric units.
5 · Radar. The other systems are for words or messages.
6 · Humber is the name of a bridge and the others are types of bridges.   7 · Renault is a French company and the others are German.   8 · Duck-billed platypus. The others are marsupials and carry their young in a pouch.   9 · Slug. The others have shells.
10 · Apollo. The others are planets.   11 · Emulsion. The others are types of paper.   12 · Iron. The others are gases.
13 · Madeira. The others are types of biscuit.   14 · Stethoscope. The others are held to the eye.   15 · Lemonade. The others are types of water.   16 · 16. The others are multiples of 9.
17 · Diamond. The others are precious metals.   18 · Jumbo. The others are famous railway engines.   19 · EEC. The other abbreviations are connected with computers.   20 · Earthworm. The others all fly.

## 48 Musical Beasts

1 · Teddy bears.   2 · Hippopotami.   3 · Nellie the elephant.   4 · Frogs in 'Rupert and the Frog Song' by Paul McCartney.   5 · Puff, the magic dragon.   6 · Crocodile.
7 · Rudolph.   8 · Chameleon.   9 · Ant.   10 · A mole.
11 · Baloo, the bear, in the film *The Jungle Book*.   12 · The Beatles.   13 · The weasel.   14 · The lion and the unicorn.
15 · Boomtown Rats.   16 · The birds, in *Feed the Birds* from *Mary Poppins*.   17 · Goosey Goosey Gander.   18 · Alligator.
19 · Mice.   20 · Doggy.

## 49 Search Party

1 · Spider.   2 · Sun.   3 · Ship.   4 · Sea.
5 · Seagulls.   6 · Submarine.   7 · Spade.   8 · Shells.
9 · Skirting board.   10 · Stars.   11 · Shoes.
12 · Satchel.   13 · Socks.   14 · Shorts.   15 · Shirt.
16 · Sunglasses.   17 · Sweets.   18 · Smoke.
19 · Saucer.   20 · Shelf.

## 50 Don't Vegetate!

1 · Beans.   2 · A potato.   3 · An onion.   4 · A permanently swollen ear.   5 · Giving away a secret.   6 · An aubergine.   7 · A Scottish scarecrow in a potato field.
8 · Cabbage Patch dolls.   9 · Left-over cloth, a perk of the trade.   10 · The leek.   11 · A German dish of chopped pickled cabbage.   12 · A pea.   13 · Carrots.   14 · Lettuce.
15 · Pumpkin.   16 · Spinach.   17 · An artichoke.   18 · A fried dish of potatoes and vegetables.   19 · A leek.   20 · A chilli!

## 51 Dining Out

1 · Haggis for the Scottish footballer.   2 · Chilli con carne for the Mexican footballer.   3 · Roast beef for the English cricketer.
4 · Pumpkin pie for the American tennis player.   5 · Sauerkraut

for the tennis player from Germany.   **6** · Irish stew for the
goalkeeper from Northern Ireland.   **7** · Samosas for the cricketer
from Pakistan.   **8** · Lasagne for the Italian footballer.
**9** · Paella for the Spanish golfer.   **10** · Quiche Lorraine for the
French racing driver.   **11** · Curds and whey.   **12** · Slices of
quince.   **13** · Spinach surprise.   **14** · Jam tarts.   **15** · Plum
pudding.   **16** · Extract of malt.   **17** · Jelly babies.
**18** · Roasted grasshoppers.   **19** · Fudge Mallow Delight.
**20** · Snozzcumbers and frobscottle.

### 52 All in the Game

**1** · Tiddly-winks.   **2** · Happy Families.   **3** · Flat-green
bowls.   **4** · Nine- or ten-pin bowling.   **5** · Bingo or lotto.
**6** · Poker.   **7** · Mah-jong.   **8** · Snakes and ladders.
**9** · One.   **10** · A single piece on a point.   **11** · A double
six.   **12** · On the black squares.   **13** · White.   **14** · 180
(three darts in the treble 20).   **15** · Chess.   **16** · Draughts.
**17** · Cluedo.   **18** · Monopoly.   **19** · Scrabble.   **20** · Trivial
Pursuit.

### 53 Togetherness

**1** · They are all bears.   **2** · They are the Railway Children in the
book by E. Nesbit.   **3** · They are all pigs.   **4** · They are all
wizards.   **5** · They are all dogs.   **6** · They are all in books by
Charles Dickens.   **7** · They are all pirates.   **8** · They are all cats
in poems by T. S. Eliot.   **9** · They are all engines in the stories by
the Revd W. Awdry.   **10** · They are all prizewinners in *Charlie and
the Chocolate Factory* by Roald Dahl.   **11** · The Beatles.
**12** · Frankie Goes to Hollywood.   **13** · Queen.   **14** · A-ha.
**15** · Bananarama.   **16** · Five Star.   **17** · Thomson Twins.
**18** · Duran Duran.   **19** · Abba.   **20** · Eurythmics.

### 54 Find the Number

**1** · 9.   **2** · 3.   **3** · 12.   **4** · 15.   **5** · 20.   **6** · 2.
**7** · 11.   **8** · 6.   **9** · 18.   **10** · 7.   **11** · 1.   **12** · 4.

**13** · 5.　**14** · 8.　**15** · 10.　**16** · 16.　**17** · 19.
**18** · 13.　**19** · 17.　**20** · 14.

## 55 Get the Point?

**1** · North Sea.　**2** · North wind.　**3** · North star.
**4** · North Pole.　**5** · Northumberland.　**6** · *EastEnders*.
**7** · East Anglia.　**8** · Middle East.　**9** · East Berlin.
**10** · Far East.　**11** · South Pacific.　**12** · South Fork.
**13** · South Atlantic.　**14** · South America.　**15** · *South Bank Show*.　**16** · Go West.　**17** · Wild West.
**18** · Westminster.　**19** · West Point.　**20** · West Germany.

## 56 Twenty Answers from Outer Space

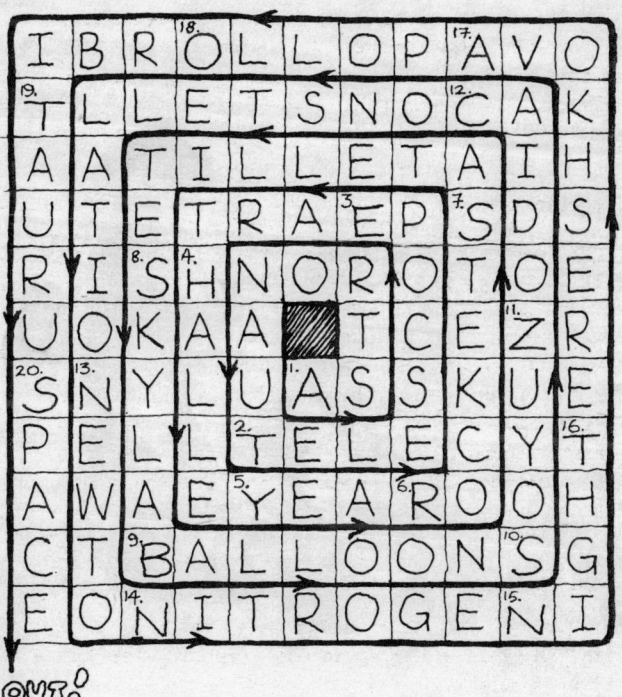

## 58 Headline News

1 · Battle of Hastings, in which King Harold died.   2 · The Magna Carta was sealed.   3 · Lady Jane Grey was deposed.
4 · Mary, Queen of Scots, was beheaded.   5 · Spanish Armada was defeated.   6 · Guy Fawkes's plot was discovered.
7 · Pilgrims sailed from Plymouth in the *Mayflower*.   8 · Charles I was beheaded.   9 · Great Fire of London began.   10 · Dick Turpin was hanged.   11 · Boston Tea Party.   12 · Mutiny on the *Bounty*.   13 · George Washington became the first president.   14 · Battle of Waterloo.   15 · Great Exhibition was opened.   16 · Stanley met Livingstone at Lake Tang at Ujiji.
17 · Scott reached the South Pole to find Amundsen had got there first.   18 · Mount Everest was first climbed.
19 · J. F. Kennedy was assassinated.   20 · First man stepped on the moon.


## 59 Up Front

1 · Fish.   2 · Bread.   3 · Toffee.   4 · Ice.
5 · Tooth.   6 · Water.   7 · Custard.   8 · Goal.
9 · Hand.   10 · Book.   11 · Cat.   12 · Foot.
13 · Flower.   14 · Sand.   15 · School.   16 · Light.
17 · King.   18 · Fly.   19 · Bird.   20 · Snow.


## 60 A Quiz to Make You Tremble

1 · Three.   2 · a).   3 · In the middle of their foreheads.
4 · c).   5 · b).   6 · c).   7 · a).   8 · By creating a whirlpool that dragged them down.   9 · It was not given a name.   10 · a).   11 · b).   12 · c).   13 · A lion's head.   14 · Their victims' necks, from which they sucked blood.   15 · c).   16 · c).   17 · Scotland.   18 · c).
19 · a).   20 · b).

The hidden monster is THE ABOMINABLE SNOWMAN.

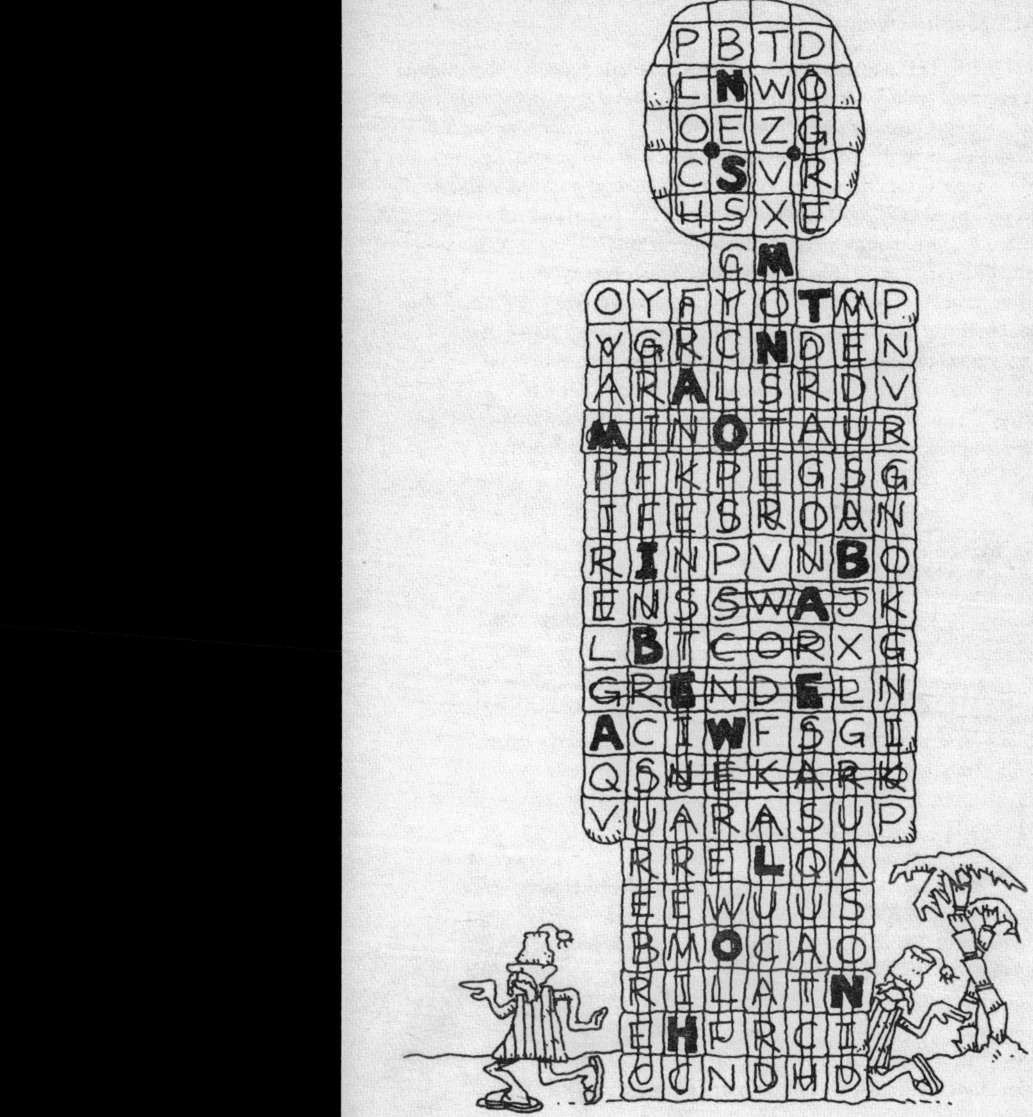
PBTD
LNWO
OEZG
CSVR
HSXE
GM
OYFYOTMP
YGRCNDEN
ARALSRDV
MINOTAUR
PFKPEGSG
IFESROAN
RINPVNBO
ENSSWAJK
LBTCORXG
GRENDELN
ACIWFSGI
QSNEKARK
VUARASUP
RRELQA
EEWUUS
BMOCAO
RILATN
EHPRCI
CCNDHD

## 61 For Wild Things

1 · False. The name means on 100 legs, but centipedes have anything from under 20 to over 150 pairs of legs.   2 · False. They can be white or purplish as well.   3 · True. Leaves of the Broad-leaved Dock, when rubbed into a sting, may relieve it.   4 · True.
5 · True.   6 · True.   7 · False. It is a fungus and gives off a strong smell to attract flies.   8 · True. A white starch was made from its roots. The plant, also called Lords-and-Ladies, is very poisonous.   9 · True, but they don't do it very often.
10 · False. Only females bite.   11 · False. A farrier is a blacksmith.   12 · False. It is called a set.   13 · False. It is a poisonous fungus.   14 · False. It is a type of butterfly.
15 · True – and it may require hospital treatment.   16 · False. They do not sting at all.   17 · False. It is the frothy protection of the froghopper larvae.   18 · False. It is a type of rodent.
19 · False. She is called a vixen.   20 · True.

## 62 Mixed Doubles

1 · Jayne Torvill and Christopher Dean. In 1984 they became European, Olympic and World Champions!   2 · Tweedledum and Tweedledee.   3 · The lion and the unicorn.   4 · Phineas T. Barnum and James A. Bailey.   5 · Charles Rolls and Frederick Royce.   6 · Paul McCartney and John Lennon.   7 · Simon Marks and Tom Spencer.   8 · William Gilbert and Arthur Sullivan.   9 · Romulus and Remus.   10 · Dr David Livingstone and Sir Henry Stanley.   11 · Sir Edmund Hillary and Sherpa Tenzing.   12 · Dr Jekyll and Mr Hyde.   13 · David and Elizabeth Emanuel.   14 · Jack and Jill.   15 · Sherlock Holmes and Dr Watson.   16 · Queen Victoria and Prince Albert.
17 · Norris and Ross McWhirter.   18 · Hansel and Gretel.
19 · George Michael and Andrew Ridgely.   20 · Annie and Clarabel.

## 63 Signs of the Times

1 · H.   2 · L.   3 · R.   4 · I.   5 · T.   6 · F.

7 · Q.    8 · J.    9 · N.    10 · A.    11 · S.    12 · O.
13 · G.    14 · K.    15 · B.    16 · E.    17 · D.
18 · P.    19 · M.    20 · C.

## 64 A Winner Every Time

1 · Football.    2 · Rugby Union (between England and Scotland).    3 · Golf.    4 · Sailing.    5 · Football.
6 · Tennis.    7 · Boxing.    8 · Horse racing.    9 · Cricket (between England and Australia).    10 · Tennis.    11 · b).
12 · The Duke of Edinburgh.    13 · One million.    14 · c) – the Academy's librarian thought that the statuette looked like her Uncle Oscar and the name stuck!    15 · 3–2–1.    16 · a).
17 · Liners – for crossing in the fastest time.    18 · c).
19 · *Blankety Blank*.    20 · b).

## 65 Let's Get Physical

1 · False. You toe the line in just six months!    2 · True.
3 · False. It's in the ear.    4 · False. It's replaced every fifty days.    5 · True.    6 · True.    7 · False. An adult has 206 bones and over 100 joints.    8 · True.    9 · False. It speeds up in the summer!    10 · True!    11 · False. It can go twice as fast as that – up to sixty m.p.h.    12 · True. That's the weight of about seven elephants!    13 · True.    14 · False, but it can rise from 70 to 200 beats.    15 · True.    16 · True.    17 · True.
18 · False. It contains 3,000!    19 · True.    20 · False. The average adult body contains six litres of blood.

## 66 Score Bored?

1 · The Prime Minister.    2 · Noah's ark.    3 · Anne, Charlotte and Emily Brontë.    4 · Salt, sweet, sour and bitter.
5 · Limericks.    6 · Liverpool – the Walton sisters.    7 · Red, orange, yellow, green, blue, indigo, violet.    8 · Great Britain.
9 · Jupiter.    10 · The decathlon.    11 · The Chancellor of the Exchequer.    12 · Grouse shooting. It's probably not so glorious for the grouse!    13 · The Stars and Stripes of America.

14 · Golf.   15 · Rugby football.   16 · Abraham Lincoln.
17 · Smiling. Frowning uses many more!   18 · Twenty-five per cent.   19 · Joan of Arc.   20 · Rip Van Winkle in the story by Washington Irving.

## 67 Twenty Bright Ideas

1 · Christmas crackers.   2 · The safety pin.   3 · Frozen food.   4 · The domestic sewing machine.   5 · The safety razor.   6 · Belisha beacon.   7 · The safety match.
8 · Dynamite.   9 · X-rays.   10 · The permanent wave.
11 · a).   12 · c).   13 · b).   14 · c).   15 · a).
16 · c).   17 · b).   18 · a).   19 · c).   20 · b).

## 68 On Safari

1 · Lions – the only big cats that hunt as a team.   2 · a) Elephants have large appetites!   3 · b).   4 · A cheetah. It can run at over ninety-five k.p.h. in short bursts.   5 · All have the same! The giraffe's are just bigger!   6 · No difference, except in the colouring, and a black panther can have light-coloured offspring.
7 · Yes. Their two-toed feet have strong toenails, which they use in fighting.   8 · A termite mound.   9 · Not bone or horn, but keratin, which may come unravelled and look like tufts of hair!
10 · They would bleed slightly and then grow back again.   11 · In young buffalo the horns are straight; they grow curved with age.
12 · They all eat carrion (dead animals).   13 · It is distributing its dung over a wide area to mark its territory and intimidate challengers!   14 · b) and c) – the air cools the mouth where the skin is thinner and the spur-winged plover does the nerve-racking dentistry.   15 · Yes, in a special pouch.   16 · It is picking up scent particles in the air and passing them to 'smelling' organs in the roof of its mouth.   17 · A chameleon.   18 · Gorillas. A silverback is a mature male.   19 · A mandrill.   20 · An aardvark.

## 69 Round the World

1 · Panama. It is a country and the others are American states.
2 · Old Faithful. It is a geyser and the others are volcanoes.
3 · New York. It is not a capital city.   4 · Amazon. It is a river and the others are canals.   5 · Mediterranean. It is a sea and the others are oceans.   6 · Gulf Stream. It is an ocean current and the others are winds.   7 · Nile. It is an African river and the others are South American.   8 · Cod. It is a cape and the others are bays.
9 · Antarctic. It is the region around the South Pole, the others are round the North.   10 · Osaka. It is in Japan and the others are in China.   11 · Pampas. They are plains in Argentina and the others are deserts.   12 · Yugoslavia. It has a coastline and the others are land-locked.   13 · Superior. It is a lake and the others are waterfalls.   14 · Rocky Mountains. They rise above their surroundings and the others are lower than them!   15 · CD. The plate indicates that the car belongs to a member of the Diplomatic Corps, while the others indicate the driver's country of origin.
16 · India. It is a subcontinent, the others are continents.
17 · Canary Islands. They are in the Atlantic and the others are in the Pacific.   18 · St Lawrence is a sea-way and the others are lakes.   19 · Cotopaxi. It is a volcano and the others are non-volcanic mountains.   20 · Wellington. It is in New Zealand and the others are in Australia.


## 70 In Their Own Words

1 · a).   2 · c).   3 · b).   4 · c).   5 · b).   6 · Winston Churchill.   7 · Napoleon.   8 · Lord Nelson.   9 · Francis Drake.   10 · Duke of Wellington.   11 · Winnie-the-Pooh in the book by A. A. Milne.   12 · Alice in *Alice's Adventures in Wonderland* by Lewis Carroll.   13 · Toad in *The Wind in the Willows* by Kenneth Grahame.   14 · Cap'n Flint in *Treasure Island* by Robert Louis Stevenson.   15 · Mr Bumble in *Oliver Twist* by Charles Dickens.   16 · Beethoven.   17 · Anne Boleyn.   18 · Julius Caesar.   19 · Lawrence Oates of Captain Scott's South Pole expedition.   20 · Lord Palmerston.